797,885 Books

are available to read at

www.ForgottenBooks.com

Forgotten Books' App
Available for mobile, tablet & eReader

ISBN 978-1-332-87666-2
PIBN 10296767

This book is a reproduction of an important historical work. Forgotten Books uses state-of-the-art technology to digitally reconstruct the work, preserving the original format whilst repairing imperfections present in the aged copy. In rare cases, an imperfection in the original, such as a blemish or missing page, may be replicated in our edition. We do, however, repair the vast majority of imperfections successfully; any imperfections that remain are intentionally left to preserve the state of such historical works.

Forgotten Books is a registered trademark of FB &c Ltd.
Copyright © 2015 FB &c Ltd.
FB &c Ltd, Dalton House, 60 Windsor Avenue, London, SW19 2RR.
Company number 08720141. Registered in England and Wales.

For support please visit www.forgottenbooks.com

1 MONTH OF
FREE
READING

at

www.ForgottenBooks.com

By purchasing this book you are eligible for one month membership to ForgottenBooks.com, giving you unlimited access to our entire collection of over 700,000 titles via our web site and mobile apps.

To claim your free month visit:

www.forgottenbooks.com/free296767

* Offer is valid for 45 days from date of purchase. Terms and conditions apply.

English
Français
Deutsche
Italiano
Español
Português

www.forgottenbooks.com

Mythology Photography **Fiction**
Fishing Christianity **Art** Cooking
Essays Buddhism Freemasonry
Medicine **Biology** Music **Ancient**
Egypt Evolution Carpentry Physics
Dance Geology **Mathematics** Fitness
Shakespeare **Folklore** Yoga Marketing
Confidence Immortality Biographies
Poetry **Psychology** Witchcraft
Electronics Chemistry History **Law**
Accounting **Philosophy** Anthropology
Alchemy Drama Quantum Mechanics
Atheism Sexual Health **Ancient History**
Entrepreneurship Languages Sport
Paleontology Needlework Islam
Metaphysics Investment Archaeology
Parenting Statistics Criminology
Motivational

Sister
Benigna Consolata
Ferrero

A Professed Choir Nun of the

Order of the Visitation, B. V. M.
COMO, ITALY

OR

"THE TENDERNESSES OF THE LOVE OF JESUS FOR A LITTLE SOUL."

fra tre ... di Sa

PUBLISHED FOR

Georgetown Visitation Convent
WASHINGTON, D. C.

BX4705
.F43C6

𝔑𝔦𝔥𝔦𝔩 𝔒𝔟𝔰𝔱𝔞𝔱:

   J<small>OSEPH</small> B<small>RUNEAU</small>, S.S., D.D.,
         Censor Deputatis.

𝔍𝔪𝔭𝔯𝔦𝔪𝔞𝔱𝔲𝔯:

   J<small>AMES</small> C<small>ARDINAL</small> G<small>IBBONS</small>
     Archbishop of Baltimore.

Baltimore, January 2, 1921.

  A<small>BBIAMO</small> veduto ed esaminato l'opusculo e, non solo me permettiamo la stampa, ma lo raccomandiamo per la maggiore diffusione in gran pro delle anime.
         + A<small>LFONSO</small> V<small>ESCOVO</small>.

C<small>OMO</small>, Agosto 1918.

———

Copyright, Sisters of the Visitation,
Georgetown, Washington, D. C.

Ⓒ Cl. A 611475

APR -4 1921

A Brief Sketch of the Life and Virtues

OF OUR DEAR SISTER

Benigna Consolata Ferrero

DECEASED IN OUR MONASTERY OF THE VISITATION, B. V. M.

of COMO, LOMBARDY,

SEPTEMBER 1, 1916, AGED 31 YEARS AND 25 DAYS:

OF RELIGIOUS PROFESSION, 6 YEARS, 9 MONTHS AND 7 DAYS,

OF THE RANK OF CHOIR SISTERS

Blessed is the man whom thou shalt instruct, O Lord:
and shalt teach him out of thy law.—Ps. XCIII. 12.

———

TRANSLATED FROM THE

Community Circular of Como

BY

FOREWORD.

In the life of Sister Benigna Consolata Ferrero, the saintly Visitandine of Como, Italy, we have a model of pure, beautiful childhood, maidenhood, and later, of extraordinary sanctity in the religious life. From her early years we witness a condescending familiarity on the part of Jesus Christ that would challenge our faith had He not said, "My delights are to be with the children of men;" had He not annihilated Himself even to the death of the Cross for each individual soul; had He not, in giving us His Sacred Heart as a new pledge of His tenderness, *uttered His heart-rending cry of love for souls and His ineffable longing for their love in return.*

The heavenly descents of the God-Man toward His creatures should not surprise us. Yet at every page of this wonderful story of "The Delicacies and Tendernesses of the Love of Jesus for a Little Soul." we are awed into silence, transported, as it were, into a celestial atmosphere, where, like Mary, we are at the feet of Jesus listening to His Gospel of sanctity.

And these pages present to us the amazing spectacle, in our own degenerate days, of a maiden who at twelve years could immolate herself as a victim of love to God, ready to suffer all privations, all tortures of mind and body, yea, to be the sport of the powers of hell, even, if she might but console the Heart of the Redeemer of the world by helping to win it back to Him—this world gone so far astray.

To what sublime heights of mystical knowledge Jesus uplifted her soul! And to corresponding depths of humiliation He lowered her! He summoned her to ever-varying modes of sacrifice, opened to her deserts of temptation where, plunged in a desolation of heart that became more intense, and yet more desirable, as divine love grew more seraphic, Sister Benigna Consolata became ravished with suffering, and sought only to share the very agonies of the Crucified.

To renounce nature at every moment, at every breath of life, was not enough; creatures must lend their aid, and in a thousand ways lacerating to the sensitive heart, help on the great work of sanctification; nay, the powers of darkness will be permitted to approach and assault her spirit, still in its baptismal innocence, and with terrors unspeakable, invading even her wasted physical frame, will strive to wrest her from the Heart of her Divine Spouse.

Yet did not Jesus Himself, after the glorious apparition of the Spirit-Dove in the opened Heavens, and the Voice of His Heavenly Father proclaiming His Divine Mission, suffer the temptations of His fiendish enemy? Did He not allow Him even a transient possession of His Sacred Person? So shall we wonder or tremble or be scandalized when, with His "Little Secretary, the Apostle of His Mercy," we pass from the fragrant airs of Paradise—her Solemn Profession with Love—to the deadly atmosphere of the enemy of all good, to her last struggle with her satanic lifelong foe?

In these Colloquies we are matriculating in a truly Divine School. The mystical life of union with God and the sure, safe and speedy means of reaching it, are taught us in the very terms of simplicity with which Jesus spoke to His disciples when He walked the roadsides or sat on the mountain slopes of Judea. And the rays of His Mercy stream from every page for the most grievous sinners who will come trusting to Him as to a divine Brother.

Our Lord is glorifying in a marvellous manner Sister Benigna Consolata, whose interior life with Jesus on earth was so secret, so hidden, so guarded even from the dear Sisters who were her daily companions, that only after her blessed death was the stupendous revelation given them by the Mother Superior who had so ably guided her and by the Ecclesiastical Superiors whose direction had ever been marked by supernatural light and prudence. Jesus had willed this profound secrecy. "Only after your death shall your writings be known," He repeatedly promised her.

This Life tells us that we have saints with us always. The Past is shining with its aureoles, as multitudinous as the stars of heaven. But the Present, too, is weaving aureoles, and gloriously, from the rays of sanctity spread over the world—in the hearts of little ones, in hearts growing seraphic in the shadow of the Tabernacle, in hearts, armed with weapons forged on Calvary, now fighting the enemies of Christ—the world and the flesh—and defying the great arch-enemy with the Cross which conquered him.

Is one of these aureoles yours?

M. S. PINE.

SISTER BENIGNA CONSOLATA FERRERO

THE "LITTLE SECRETARY OF JESUS"

(1885-1916)

𝕺𝖓𝖑𝖞 𝖙𝖍𝖊 𝖆𝖈𝖙𝖎𝖔𝖓𝖘 𝖔𝖋 𝖙𝖍𝖊 𝕵𝖚𝖘𝖙
𝕾𝖒𝖊𝖑𝖑 𝖘𝖜𝖊𝖊𝖙 𝖆𝖓𝖉 𝖇𝖑𝖔𝖘𝖘𝖔𝖒 𝖎𝖓 𝖙𝖍𝖊 𝖉𝖚𝖘𝖙.

I

BIRTH OF MARIA CONSOLATA; HER CHILDHOOD AND EARLY YOUTH.

It is with feelings of indescribable emotion that we undertake to write the incomparable life of our angelic Sister Benigna Consolata. To our great regret, we can give only an imperfect idea of the beauty of this privileged soul so tenderly beloved by the Divine Master, who in His intimate and continual colloquies with His little spouse, named her familiarly the Benjamin of His Heart. Ever docile in listening to the divine voice, her eyes constantly fixed on the Heart of her God, so good, so tender, so merciful, our beloved Sister attained, in a very short time, to the highest perfection, so that the Divine Spouse, looking upon her with complacency, could say to her: "Thy heart is a garden inclosed to Me, a Paradise in which I take my delights."

Our dear Sister was born in Turin on August 6, 1885, the Feast of the Transfiguration of Our Lord, of distinguished and very pious parents,—Signor Sebastiano Ferrero and Signora Carolina Pansa. On the following day, the Feast of St. Gaetano, she received the grace of Baptism, with the names Maria, Consolata, Rosalia, Theresa, Philomena and Gaetano. Her god-father, Ignatius Barbesio, was a fervent Catholic, as well as her god-mother, Signora Rosalia Bertagna, a pious widow.

If the happy birth of the sweet infant gave joy to the family, the Angels on high must have contemplated with pleasure her who had already been named their sister. The beautiful name of Maria

Consolata was, as it were, a happy presage of what she was to become later—the sweet consoler of the Heart of Jesus. We doubt not that Our Lord Himself suggested the names He wished for His future spouse.

Signora Ferrero, to her great regret, was obliged to intrust her dear treasure to a nurse in the vicinity of Turin. Suffering made no delay in marking our little one with its seal; her nourishment was insufficient to preserve health, and she declined from day to day. Fortunately, her mother perceived it; in great distress yet placing all her confidence in God, she repaired, full of faith, to the Church of St. Dalmazzo, and kneeling before the altar of Our Lady of Loretto, prayed fervently for assistance and counsel from the Immaculate Virgin. She who was never invoked in vain showed as usual her power and goodness; and the sweet babe, transferred to the care of another nurse, soon regained strength and health.

When Maria was fourteen months old, Signora Ferrero took her home and lavished upon her all the care and attention of her maternal loving heart. She beheld this pure Lily, which already captivated the eyes of Jesus, grow and flourish daily. The pious and vigilant mother rarely left her little Maria, and then only to intrust her to her own sister, Signora Rosalia, or to a servant of tried fidelity.

Having attained the age of five years, Maria began to attend the common school. The first year she went alone. Afterward her younger sister Adeline became her faithful companion. The latter, deprived of the maternal caresses, fell into a kind of agony on arriving at school, shedding such a deluge of tears that no one could calm or console her but Maria, whose sweet and tender words overflowed from a heart full of affection' and compassion.

Three years later Signora Ferrero, desiring to secure for her children a good education and have them worthily prepared for their First Communion, placed them in the boarding-school of the Sisters of St. Joseph. Thenceforward Adeline became more and more the object of the care and tenderness of her elder sister; for the Academy being at some distance from her home, the little girls were entered as half-boarders. "Maria Consolata," said Adeline, "divined my little trials, and knew how to cheer away my melancholy; indeed she watched over me with all the kindness of my dear mamma."

We know nothing of the first meeting of the Eucharistic Jesus with the privileged child of His Heart. But how can we doubt

8

that the Divine Master gave His first kiss to His future spouse with ineffable tenderness, and that, on this blessed day, He took full possession of that heart which was to correspond so fully to His love? We have two copy-books containing summaries of sermons, entitled: "Souvenir of Holy Exercises Preparatory to my First Communion." These pages are written in the small hand of a child; the writing is beautiful, the style flowing, the thought elevated and touched with a ravishing simplicity. She names these pages her "Spiritual Edifice." Below this title we read the following prayer: "O good Jesus, come into my poor heart, come and help me raise my spiritual edifice; build it so well that it may merit to be placed by Thee one day in the celestial Jerusalem." It was during the same year that Maria received the Sacrament of Confirmation.

Blessed are those who had the honor and happiness of preparing the angelic maiden for her first interview with the Spouse of virgins, and who directed her so young into the ways of sanctity. The Lord had such marvelous designs over this soul! Our dear Sister ever kept a faithful remembrance of her pious teachers and alludes to them in her writings with loving gratitude.

Maria returned afterward to finish her studies in the common school, where her application won for her notable success. On Thursday, the weekly holiday, she went to receive religious instruction. Although still very young, her upright soul was avid of the divine Word: she studied the catechism with her whole soul, and meditated lovingly upon it in silence and recollection. Her excellent teacher, Signora Capra, had promised to give a prize at the end of the year to the best pupil in the class. But in order to deserve it a rigorous silence was enjoined. This was a hard trial for little girls of that age. "Cost what it will," said Maria Consolata, "I must obtain the prize." Later in relating this fact to our Honored Mother, she added; "O dear Mother, if you only knew what violence I had to do myself in order to keep silence! Sometimes I was seized with such a desire to speak that I bit my tongue to prevent my yielding to the temptation."

Maria Consolata was about to terminate her classes with honor when Signora Ferrero, hearing that a Lyceum for young girls was opened in our city (Como), placed her dear child there in order that she might complete her studies. Unforeseen circumstances caused the closing of this establishment at the end of a few months. She was then placed under the care of the Ladies of the Institute of the Sacred Heart at Turin. There her rare virtues began to attract attention. Not only was her conduct irreproachable, but so edifying that her teachers feared not to propose her as a model to all her companions. Far from experiencing vanity over it, her modesty was so perfect, her humility so sincere, that one would have said there was question of the praise of another. One day her professor, seized with admiration at the beauty and precision of a drawing, said to her before every one: "I would like to place by your side a phonograph which would repeat continually: "Brava! Brava!" (Excellent! Excellent!) Maria Consolata, in no wise elated, pursued her task tranquilly in her own sweet way.

While her beautiful intellect was being enriched with useful and varied knowledge, her soul was assuredly not neglected. Continuing to assist weekly at the courses of religious instruction, Maria Consolata felt her faith become more and more lively and the flame of her charity more and more ardent. To visit Jesus in His Sacrament of Love was her sweetest happiness, and her colloquies with Our Lord in the Holy Tabernacle fertilized the precious seed cast into her young heart with profusion and preserved by our beloved Sister with such rare fidelity. To converse with the Divine Prisoner was her favorite exercise; hence she arose very early in the morning to go to Church. One year her family went into the country to pass the summer; the church was very far from the hotel, and the dear child, who burned with desire to receive her God, had to content herself frequently with a spiritual communion. This was a painful sacrifice; but she said not a word, uttered not a complaint. viewing in this as in all things the adorable Will of God. To indemnify herself, however, she devoted her time to good works, collected offerings for poor churches and orphanages, and endeavored with all her power to shed around her devotion to the Blessed Virgin and the Saints.

Our dear Sister knew nothing of human respect. During the summer while boarding in the hotel, she never failed to make the Sign of the Cross and say the Benedicite before the repast and Grace at the end. All eyes were fixed upon her, but she took no notice of it. However, her sweet piety at last attracted the admiration of all present, and one very distinguished lady followed her example.

Maria had an absolute aversion for worldly amusements and often deprived herself of the most innocent pleasures, loved by those of her age; but like all great souls the contemplation of nature captivated her; hence her greatest happiness was to make an excursion into the mountains. Later, when a religious, while admiring the beauty of the mountains of Lombardy which encircle our Monastery, she would recall the joyous parties which she had formerly shared on the hills of Turin; and all in smiles, her hands joined in the attitude of prayer common to her, she would say: "O how pure were those pleasures!" Once she ascended two hundred and sixty steps leading to a Sanctuary dedicated to the Blessed Virgin, and situated in a little Alpine village in the midst of rocks and precipices. But her piety was so ardent that one would have said she experienced neither fatigue nor weariness although the pilgrimage lasted nearly three hours. With what love the sweet Queen of heaven must have welcomed the fervent young girl, who to prove her love had feared neither the length nor the pain of the ascent!

Frequently while going for a walk to Coaze, she would pause half way, and ascending an elevated hill whence one could enjoy the splendid panorama of the whole plain of Turin, Maria Consolata would contemplate this grand tableau in mysterious silence; but her glance went far beyond it to descry, lost like a point in space, the object of her dearest aspirations, the Monastery of the Visitation of Santa-Maria.

II

FROM HER DIARY.

At what hour did our dear sister hear the Divine Call? When did Jesus name her for the first time His Joy and His Benjamin? We do not know. The first pages of her precious manuscripts are dated November, 1902; she was then about seventeen years old; but everything leads us to believe that Our Lord had spoken to her long before. "One day," she writes, "my soul felt sweetly attracted and I heard the voice of my God; it was so sweet that I scarcely dared to make a movement for fear of hearing it no longer, and while listening I wept with emotion. Jesus told me that He would give Himself to me, that He would be to me as a mother to a child, and that He would furnish me occasions of suffering for Him."

After this revelation we find recorded in her notes an incident which we think we ought to cite here, as it shows the vigilance she exercised over herself. One day having soiled her dress she was much grieved and sought at once some means of removing the ugly spot. Suddenly entering into herself she noticed that when she happened to soil her soul she was not so grieved, and her heart was filled with sadness.

About this time the Divine Master manifested His desire that she should live in the world as if she were already in the cloister, recommending her to have Him alone as the end of her life and actions; she was not to burden herself any more than possible for her neighbor, so that God might have the larger part. He explained to His beloved His mysterious "Sitio," ("*I thirst*") promising to give her a thirst for the salvation of souls which would make her avid of sufferings and humiliations. He warned her to prepare for the conflict, which would not fail her if she wished to be ever faithful to the operations of grace and to conquer her rebellious nature. Lis-

ten to her reply: "O Jesus, do with me all that Thou wilt; I place
in Thee all my confidence and I abandon myself to Thy loving cares;
henceforth I wish to serve Thee in peace, joy and love, as Thou Thyself hast taught me; but let me implore Thee to grant me the grace
of knowing Thee that I may love Thee with all my heart, and of
knowing myself that I may humble myself profoundly."

God could not resist such prayers. We shall see this verified as
we advance in our recital; and we may affirm that it was the profound contempt she had for herself that attracted to our dear Sis
ter such exceptional graces. On one occasion being tortured with
the fear of having offended Jesus He deigned Himself to reassure
her: "Take care, Maria, the demon wishes to discourage thee by
persuading thee that thou hast committed a fault; thou hast not
yielded; despise the temptation and have confidence in Me."

This delicacy of conscience our dear Sister carried even to scru
pulosity. She suffered and was afflicted at the least shadow of in
fidelity. This trial was her daily martyrdom, the more so, since,
in spite of her extreme timidity and naturally fearful disposition,
she was called to ascend rapidly the holy way of perfect confidence
in God. Every day Jesus spoke to her to instruct and fortify her.
The infinite tenderness of His Sacred Heart as well as His burning
desire to draw to Himself all hearts by the sweet bonds of confidence and love, overflows like a divine torrent in the writings
of His dear confidant. Let us listen to the Adorable Master: "I
am going to make of thy soul," He said, "a masterpiece of My
grace; take care not to interrupt its beneficent action; try to second
My inspirations and to be faithful to them. Mortify the natural taste
thou hast for so much speaking and listening; and when thou seest
that nature is getting the upper hand, do just the contrary to what
it desires in order to subject it completely to grace."

Painful aridities were generally her portion. On the other hand
the enemy of all good tortured her with terrible doubts. The divine
communications even were to her a source of anguish she had such
a fear of being deceived, and this very fear came from the demon;
but her confidence soon regained its strength so that she was never
vanquished; and with Jesus and for the love of Jesus she escaped
victorious and triumphant over the snare laid by Satan.

"Thy soul," said the Divine Master to her, "shall mature in silence, in affliction and abnegation; prepare it well, for I wish to
make it the instrument of My designs. I have chosen thee because

thou art wretched and miserable, in order that thou mayst attribute nothing to thyself and know that all good comes from God."

Yes, it was toward this *nothing* that placed in Him all her confidence that Jesus condescended with ineffable goodness. He wished to converse continually with His little spouse, who was already bound to Him by four vows, as we shall see later. He consoled her in her sufferings, and sometimes reproached her, but always with divine sweetness and gentleness.

"Maria," He said, "no longer go begging the love of creatures; were they to give themselves entirely to thee thou wouldst not be satisfied. God alone can suffice for thee. Maria, thou hast need of a heart which loves thee, which understands thee; it is the Heart of God thou needest. Speak to Me as thou wouldst to an earthly friend, to whom one tells everything. I know thee, I share thy sufferings, I offer Myself to be thy Model and on this thou must carefully form thyself. Live in such a manner that Jesus may truly live in thee and rule all thy actions, thy desires and thy will. Dost thou understand with what perfection thou shouldst act if thou wouldst manifest Jesus living and reigning in thee? Even when thou art enduring cruel interior sufferings, thy countenance must appear smiling. I desire thou shouldst be sweet and cordial toward all, but especially toward those who give thee occasions of immolation and sacrifice."

On November 16, 1902, at the beginning of a Spiritual Retreat, our dear Sister wrote with childish candor the following resolution: "I wish to become a Saint; and with the assistance of Our Lord I begin today the work of the sanctification of my soul. May all be for the greater glory of God! I must consider myself as a nothing and fight mercilessly against my nature."

The next day her Divine Spouse came to encourage her: "Thou hast taken the resolution to become holy: this is well and thou must not fail; but it is not to an ordinary sanctity thou art called; thou must aim at the most sublime perfection."

On hearing these words our dear Sister cast a glance upon her nothingness, and seized with fright she said to her good Master· "My Jesus, is it not pride and presumption on my part to aspire to an end so elevated, I who am weakness itself?"

"It would be indeed," He answered, "if thou didst depend on thy own strength; but if thou wilt hope for all from God, He will sustain thee in thy conflicts and will help thee to surmount all the obstacles that could hinder the reign of pure love in thy soul."—"I am confused and troubled," replied the humble child, "at being favored with so many graces, I who lead a life so little conformed to Thy divine will, when so many fervent souls would draw far greater profit from them."

Our dear Sister feared that the abundance of favors with which she was loaded would be to the detriment of others. Her incomparable Master, touched with this exquisite delicacy, gave her a loving instruction, showing her the entire liberty souls have in the choice of good or evil. He assured her that He invited all to choose the good by following the sweet attractions of His love; then He added: "Pray much for sinners, especially on these days that precede the Paschal Feasts, and I will grant all thou shalt ask. I place thee as an intermediary between poor sinners and thy Heavenly Spouse; plead their cause then and say to Me; My Jesus, wilt Thou let these souls be lost for whom Thou didst die on the Cross? Thou art the Resurrection and the Life: be so then to all these hearts buried so long in the darkness of death. From this time forward I shall thank Thee for the victory Thou dost gain over the infernal enemy, who held them in the slavery of sin, since Thou Thyself hast assured me that I shall obtain all I ask of Thee with confidence."

This prayer, dictated by Jesus to our dear little Sister, is the first we have found in her writings; to this precious ring will be added many others; and they will form an admirable chain of prayers all impregnated with faith and love.

"My Jesus," she wrote on March 29, "pardon me the liberty I take in speaking thus to Thee; Thou canst do all things; grant then that men may know Thee, love Thee, and serve Thee with all the respect and love Thou dost merit." And Jesus responded; "I use *creatures* for this end, making them the instruments of My Mercy. I choose Myself those souls destined to revive the Christian spirit; I form them Myself; I overload them with My graces, and so prepare them for their mission. Such souls have been in the past; they live at present; and I will raise up others in the future. Thou art one of these souls, Maria; now thou art exercising thy mission in the family; later in the Monastery, and at last thou shalt exercise it from the cloister in the world, which shall be embalmed with the sweet perfume of the virtues I am cultivating in thee with so much love."

The vocation of our dear Sister ripened more and more; she had

an irresistible attraction for our Holy Institute; the piety of her
family, the frequent reception of the Sacraments, the reading of
excellent books which Canon Boccardo lent her from her twelfth
year until her entry among us, all contributed to render her desire
of the religious life more vehement. While awaiting the means of
entering into the blessed Ark, she was the Angel of her family, their
charm and their happiness, devoting herself joyously to every kind
of duty, especially to the accounts and correspondence of the house.

Our dear Sister had two brothers, one of whom, John, a distinguished physician, gave brilliant promise for the future. She loved
him with a special love. But the Lord was about to strike a great blow
to the loving heart of His privileged child, bruising it and drawing
her entirely to Himself. John fell ill, and Maria became his self-
constituted nurse. She never left his side, lavishing upon him all
those delicate attentions and that tender devotedness which sisterly
love alone can inspire. What anguish, what fears, what sacrifices
were hers during those days of trial! She was consoled in seeing
the admirable patience and resignation of the young patient, while
his virtuous sister poured into his heart the balm of her sweet
compassion. How often she had to triumph over the revolts of nature before duties painful to accomplish! One day, imitating St.
Catherine of Siena, she conquered heroically an indescribable repugnance. O we cannot doubt that after this sublime act, Jesus,
the sweet Jesus, attracted her to His Sacred Heart and made her
drink long draughts of the sweetness of His divine tenderness!

John's heart overflowed with loving gratitude toward his charitable nurse; and often to show her how much good he derived from
her presence and holy words, he would say to her: "O you are
more necessary to me than food!" Later, when in the Monastery,
recalling these sorrowful days, our Sister wrote: "Our Lord wished
to detach me from everything, that I might be His alone. In taking
away from me that brother so beloved, He began to dig in my heart
a void which He alone could fill." In spite of the skilful care and
devotedness of his family the dear young patient declined from
day to day. With edifying piety he received the Last Sacraments
and prepared for the great journey to eternity. Maria Consolata,
calm and resigned, controlling her sorrow, read for him the act of
acceptance of death, composed by the Venerable Cafasso, desiring
to obtain for her dying brother the Plenary Indulgence. He ex_
pired peacefully in her arms, surrounded by his weeping family.

Our beloved Sister, forgetting her own sorrow, became the consoler of her good parents, and of the brother and sister who still remained.

It is to the latter we owe the interesting details of the life of Sister Benigna from her birth to her entry into our Monastery. Adeline pretended that she had been a source of suffering to her elder sister. "Being mischievous and capricious," she said, "I often caused her pain which she bore in silence." This is difficult to believe, for see what we find in the writings of our dear Sister:— "The Lord in His immense goodness gave me an angel in the person of my younger sister, with whom I passed beautiful years, delicious days at home, living one heart and one soul with my beloved Adeline". With what tenderness she spoke to us of her at the recreations! She confessed that in leaving the paternal mansion she endured a cruel conflict of soul, having a great love for her God and a tender affection for her family:—her heart was broken at the bare thought of separation; and on the other hand she burned with desire to shut herself up in the Cloister.

Jesus did not forsake her. He was ever near her attracting her to Himself with infinite delicacy by His sweet invitations. Everything in her exterior revealed the interior beauty of her soul, which the Divine Master replenished with graces and virtues. In the meantime, no one suspected that the God strong and terrible, whose glance alone makes the earth tremble and shakes the highest mountains, was condescending so benignly toward the humble child, favoring her continually with His divine conversation. Only the guide of her soul, Canon Boccardo, was her confidant. Maria opened her heart to him with infantine candor; and it is to this worthy priest we owe the happiness of possessing her first writings, commencing in 1902, as we have said, and continued until her coming among us. Struck at once with admiration and astonishment at beholding the marvellous progress of his penitent in the way of perfection, enchanted at seeing her so humble, so obedient, the wise Director, under pretext of knowing better what passed within her, ordered her to write all that the "Voice" said to her. "In reality," he confessed, "I wished to nourish my soul with the delicious food served by the infinitely good God to His privileged child, and relish it at my ease."

Maria was conscious of a great repugnance on receiving this obedience, but, humbly and submissively, she set herself to work at once to accomplish it. Her multiplied occupations left her little leisure;

and we cannot but wonder how she was able to perform a task of such magnitude, and this unknown to all around her, as she had been wisely counselled. We have under our eyes hundreds of pages the greater part of which is written in pencil without correction or erasure. One can perceive neither haste nor apprehension; and yet she had to be ingenious and exercise continual watchfulness in order to hide herself from all eyes. But Jesus was there. Taking more and more possession of her whole being, He aided her, guarding her visibly, revealing to her the future, and granting her the gift of discernment of spirits. These exceptional gifts, we repeat, became the torment of the poor child, who, naturally timid, was frightened at such extraordinary ways, sometimes so dangerous. Happily she had unlimited confidence in her Spiritual Father; her obedience became her buckler—her defense against the enemy who had already sworn an implacable hatred to the little favorite of Jesus.

Let us return now to the journal of our dear Sister, and we shall relish together the divine teachings of the Master; we shall penetrate more deeply into the soul of His beloved, and, discovering there the treasures of His graces, bless Him for so many marvels. As to ourselves, who had the happiness of receiving her into our Community and living in her angelic company, we can never cease offering to God our humble gratitude.

On April 3, 1903, Maria prepared to make a general Confession, so to correspond to the desire of Jesus. He asked her which she would prefer—the gift of sensible consolation and the grace to weep over her sins, or perfect renunciation of every satisfaction in order to obtain the conversion of a sinner. "O Jesus", she answered, "take away everything; I desire only Thee and Thy glory! If this will be useful to that soul and to others, take away from me every consolation; I sacrifice all to Thee; let the enemy tempt me; let him make me believe that I am lost; that I am an object of hatred in Thy eyes; let him torture my soul with vain fears for involuntary faults;— I accept all. I implore only Thy grace that I may not offend Thee in this painful state, through lack of confidence in Thy infinite goodness. It will be a sweet balm to the wounds of my heart to know that Thine is consoled by the return of so many wandering souls. O may they be numerous, my Jesus!"

And Jesus accepted the generous immolation. The state that His privileged spouse has just described will be, as it were, the history of her life, intermingled, like that of her predecessor, our Blessed Sister Saint Margaret Mary, with indescribable sweetnesses; but more frequently cruel torments will be her portion.

Let us listen again:—"I am sometimes so oppressed with sorrow, so troubled through the fear of not corresponding with God's grace, that I can scarcely trust in His goodness. It is principally in prayer that my sufferings are augmented: while there I ought not and wish not to be mindful of aught but God; but alas! all sorts of thoughts present themselves to my mind. The demon, delighted, takes hold of the occasion to torment me. Overwhelmed, I am tempted to leave off prayer through dread of making it badly; but I do not yield, and continue in spite of suffering. If I could tell my sufferings to some one it seems to me I should be relieved; but God alone knows these interior pains. When I would manifest my state to my Director, I have so slight a remembrance of it that I cannot find terms to express myself; for these are spiritual sufferings that at times I myself cannot comprehend."

The devotion to the Sacred Heart of Jesus was her great attraction; in that profoundly religious family, the picture of the Sacred Heart, placed in honor in the dining-hall, was the special charge of the pious Maria; she decorated it with passionate love. In the beautiful month of June all the flowers in the garden were for Him, and a light burned before the little shrine continually. Irresistibly drawn toward her God, Maria one day, believing herself alone in the room, in an impetus of love which she could not restrain before a picture of the Sacred Humanity of Jesus, kissed with ardor His Sacred Feet and then His Divine Heart, saying: "With humility I go to the Feet of Jesus, and with love I go to His Sacred Heart."— The distinguished Directress of the Institute of the Sacred Heart said of her: "With each Daily Commuion the dear child made rapid progress in wisdom and virtue. Her daily program was: The sanctification of my soul and that of my neighbor; union of love with Jesus, labor and prayer."

On the 29th of April while she was a prey to extreme desolation of heart, Our Lord said to her: "Know that in those painful moments in which it seems as if the demon is about to tear thee from my Heart, thou art more closely united to Me by the strong bonds of love. Art thou not the happy prey of Love? How canst thou be afraid of the demon when the Almighty is with thee? I am the cuirass of thy soul; then fear not the blows destined for thee; a soldier fears not the snares of the enemy when he knows he is powerfully defended. And what I say to thee is not for thyself alone, but also for so many souls who are in the same state. I repeat it; I wish thee to make known to souls what I teach thee; CONFI-DENCE IS THE KEY WHICH OPENS THE TREASURES OF MY MERCY."

On May 2, he stimulated her in regard to mortification:—"I would have thee do greater penances. With the consent of thy Spiritual Father thou shalt gird thy reins with a knotted cord which will pain the flesh without awakening the suspicions of those around. Hence try to be joyous always. I shall continue to try thee by interior and exterior pains. I wish thee to attain to forgetfulness of self in everything; and I promise thee the grace of equality of humor which is so necessary to maintain thee in the practice of virtue."

Some days afterward, the 13th, her Divine Spouse asked her to make a vow to love Him with her whole heart. Terrified at her weakness Maria Consolata hesitated; but she was quickly encouraged by her dear Master, who Himself dictated to her the following formula:

"I make the vow to love my God with all my heart; and for love of Him I shall strive to love my neighbor as He has taught me."

"Thou doest this already," the Adorable Master assured her, "but I wish to oblige thee to do it ever more and more perfectly." She begged Him humbly to make Himself known to her that she might love Him as much as He desired. "Yes, I will make Myself known to thee and thou shalt love Me," He answered. "Have an affection for recollection, silence and solitude; every beginning is difficult, especially when there is question of practicing virtue; but do not be afraid; thou shalt become strong through My grace, provided thou bury thy littleness in My Mercy."

On the 21st of the same month Jesus said to her: "I desire thou shouldst honor My Divine Heart particularly during the month consecrated to It: therefore I shall awaken thee at four instead of half past four in the morning, in order to converse with thee. I shall call thee twice in the night, and each time thou shalt arise, and kneeling kiss the ground. The first time thou shalt say five times "Jesus," as My Minister has taught thee; the second time thou shalt say three times, "Jesus Crucified, crucify me with Thee." Thou shalt wear the cord during the day, adding to it two more knots; and thou shalt wear it during the night to render thy sleep painful. Do not let suffering frighten thee; thou art capable of nothing; hence

I use thee to accomplish My designs. I use the vilest and most miserable instruments that all may recognize the action of My grace."

On May 30 He again addressed her: "It is useless to try to overcome the anguish which oppresses thee: it is I who permit it. Do not struggle any longer to be recollected and absorbed in Me; it will only increase thy pain. Thou art walking in obscurity, it is true; but thou art not alone, I am with thee; abandon everything to me then, like a poor blind person who trusts in the guide with perfect confidence. I speak to thee directly, and I make use also of my devout Minister; together we shall foresee the obstacles thou mayst encounter, so that thou mayst be ever on the watch to avoid them. Follow faithfully our counsels and do not fear; that soul alone is lost who absolutely wills it in spite of the reiterated solicitations of My grace."

The Divine Heart afterward gave her a second mission, without however releasing her from the first, the salvation of sinners; He enjoined her to pray for religious souls who live in a state of tepidity. "Thou shalt pray to Me thus," He said:—"O Jesus, who hast granted to these souls the signal grace of serving Thee in a more perfect state, do not permit them to abuse so great a treasure by passing their lives in tepidity and negligence; revive in their hearts the flame of Thy love, so that repairing the past and sanctifying better the future, they may enjoy Thee in Heaven for all eternity." After these tender words, He added: "I am preparing the work of My Mercy; I desire a new resurrection of Society but it will be a work of love. I shall make use of thee to communicate Myself to My creatures, and to make known to them My Will." He inspired her with new courage in regard to the vow she had made to love Him purely for Himself, and urged her to do always what she believed to be most perfect in order to become more agreeable to Him.

· While Jesus took His delights in this soul, so pure, her interior martyrdom redoubled. Maria Consolata feared she was under illusion, and trembled at the bare thought of being unfaithful to her vows. Our Lord used her to enlighten the way of him who directed her, while she remained in thick darkness. Obedience was her pharos and her support; the love of Jesus heartened her and His sweet voice encouraged her.

"When thou art suffering," He said, "whether interiorly or exteriorly, do not lose the merit of thy pain; suffer only for Me. The greater number of souls, often even pious souls, lose much merit by relating what they suffer to anyone who will hear them; and although they do not complain, they desire no less the sympathy of creatures. When My Divine Heart sends suffering It wills that the soul accept it with patience and resignation. Such persons believe that their trials will be relieved by pouring them out to the creature; nature is satisfied, but grace is weakened, and courage fails them afterward to bear their sufferings through pure love. I am going to dictate to thee Myself the sentiments which should animate thee in the greatest trials. Thou shalt say to thy Spouse :— O Jesus, only Love of my heart, I wish to suffer what I suffer and all Thou wilt have me suffer, for Thy pure love, not because of the merits I may acquire, nor for the rewards Thou hast promised me, but only to please thee, to praise Thee, to bless Thee, as well in sorrow as in joy."

On June 20, 1903, Maria Consolata, not seeing the realization of a promise she believed God had made her, was assailed anew by terrible fears. She believed herself a victim of the delusions of the devil and doubted that it was Jesus who spoke to her; she strove, therefore, to repulse the interior "Voice". Obedience obliges her to write all that passes within her, and now she is tortured lest she should write only lies. If she writes, it is with fear and trembling; if she does not write, remorse takes possession of her soul. In this painful state she would have recourse to her Spiritual Father, but he is absent. The enemy, taking advantage of her trouble, suggests that she should omit Holy Communion, and she at once discovers the ruse of the tempter. "I know that I shall receive in Holy Communion strength to resist the wiles of the demon; therefore I will not yield and deprive myself of the Sacred Bread through motives which have no reality, but are unfounded fears. I earnestly entreat my God to deliver me from these illusions if I am truly their victim, Satan taking the appearance of an angel of light to penetrate my mind. The Lord, it is true, deigns to speak to me as heretofore, but His words leave only a momentary calm in my spirit, followed by terrible temptations. I believe the only remedy to keep peace in the midst of this tempest is to submit to all the orders of my Director; his persuasive and fatherly words will restore my tranquillity, if I follow his counsels with humility; and I will do so, with the grace of my God, *for cost what it will, I must conquer."*

While she was writing the last lines, her Beloved interrupted her, consoling her with infinite tenderness:—"Listen to Me, My spouse; it is because I love thee that I treat thee thus. The most precious gift I can make to My friends is that of the Cross. I send to the soul what costs it most, what it dreads most; this is the best means of making it advance. It is to comfort thee I speak thus; and I assure thee that thou art far from displeasing Me when thou art in this painful state, since it is I who permit it. I know what is good for thee; let Me act. I am beginning to nourish thee in thy youth with the substantial bread of sorrow, and during thy whole life I shall satiate thee abundantly with this celestial manna."

On June 24, our future Sister being still in the same state, Jesus said to her:—"Thou art in such aridity thou canst not see what passes within thee; but be tranquil, these difficulties will disappear; arm thy will! And hast thou not thy God to sustain thee and make thee triumph? O how I love to see thee combat! Therefore I shall be on My guard against freeing thee from occasions. Do not be astonished that I speak to thee so familiarly; I act thus with My children for in them I take My delights; but the greater number know not how to receive and put in practice My words of eternal life. Do thou at least receive them and put them to profit for thyself and others."

He showed her anew on the following day the value of the Cross. "Listen to Me: I am going to ask a gift of thee. Wilt thou in exchange for the infinite love I bear thee give Me a special testimony of affection? I desire thou shouldst offer it to My Divine Heart to save sinners. By joining thy works to prayer thou wilt obtain more easily what thou desirest so ardently—the salvation of souls. There is question therefore of making Me a generous sacrifice of that portion of merit which still remains to thee after the donation thou hast made in favor of the souls in Purgatory by the heroic act of charity. Nothing will remain to thee of what thou shalt do or suffer: surrender all to Me that I may dispose of it at My Will in favor of the souls whose conversion thou dost seek. This generous offering will attract to thee the choicest benedictions of God and make thee participate in the benefits of Redemption, since thou dost sacrifice all that thou art, all that thou hast, and all that thou doest, for those poor souls who, thanks to thee, will obtain mercy and pardon from My Heart. Therefore must thou have a loving and constant generosity which recoils not before the greatest sacrifices. Be holily avid not to let one pass without offering it to Me; the more thou shalt vanquish thy repugnances the more special graces thou shalt receive. Let this promise encourage thee not to tremble in the face of trial; accept it, bear it sweetly through love; and in exchange thou shalt obtain from Me all thou dost hope for, all thou canst desire."

Aridity was habitually the portion of Maria Consolata. We read in her notes of June 28, 1903:—"What I am going to write does not come from me; I am the first to recognize it. I write to please my Jesus and to assist those souls who may be in my present situation. When I am in aridity, I say to Jesus: My Divine Spouse, if Thou willest I should be in this state till my last sigh, Thy will is mine: take all—relations, goods, affections, health, honor, all. Provided Thou leave me my heart to love Thee, it is enough for me. I wish to know Thee better that I may love Thee more; I hope for this grace from Thy infinite goodness: I am certain of obtaining it, but I do not wish to hasten even by a moment the hour in which it will please Thee to grant it. If Thou shouldst tell me that by loving Thee I should augment Thy glory, and by it I should diminish mine for all eternity, I would not only love Thee as much, but even more, if it were possible."

On July 14, 1903, Our Lord said to her:—"Thou shalt make thy Purgatory in the flames of My pure love."

And five days later He traced out the program for her whole life. "Blessed is she whom God chooses to be the instrument of His mercies toward souls. But she ought not to render herself useless by her infidelities. On the contrary she ought to strive most earnestly to do everything possible to obtain new graces for herself and others. It is to thyself, O Maria, that these words are addressed. Thy mission is to do all the good thou canst to the greatest possible number of souls. A mission painful and dolorous, which will cost thee many sacrifices; but the consoling thought will be thine, that thou wilt thus increase the glory of thy God. I tell thee these things to encourage thee to suffer, because ere long thou must drink the Chalice I have prepared for thee. O my poor beloved! through how many torments I shall make thee pass in order to refine and purify thee, that there may be nothing in thee displeasing to thy God! Prepare thyself to suffer new pains and temptations, which, like frightful phantoms, will assail thy spirit. But I repeat, they will be simple phantoms, which for thy consolation the light of My Presence will dissipate in a moment. Nature will be crushed, but the spirit will live; thou wilt acquire a new vigor, and from these trials, supported with heroic patience, there will result a desire to suffer which will leave thee no repose." Turning then toward Jesus His little spouse replied: "O Jesus, my greatest happiness will always be to do Thy Will, provided Thou deignest to help me with the succors of Thy grace."

On July 21, 1903, she writes ingenuously: "Here are four resolu‧ tions I intend to present to Jesus on my birthday. I shall then be nineteen years old:—How much time lost! How many graces rendered useless! But it shall be so no longer; Maria is going to begin a new life: the Cross of Jesus will be her delight, and like a true lover, she will no longer avoid it.—1. I shall no longer seek myself. 2. I shall abandon myself totally to the care of Divine Providence, and do blindly all that my Director shall order. 3. I shall no longer speak of myself deliberately, neither of what I do, nor of what I intend to do; and if I am questioned, I will answer in such a manner as not to fail in holy humility. 4. I shall have for my neighbor that charity which knows how to compassionate and encourage at the same time; and as to what concerns myself, I shall consider contempt and disdain as a supreme good, esteeming myself too happy to have some mark of resemblance with Jesus."

We have said that Our Lord spoke to her not only for herself, but also for others: He even revealed to her the beauty and merit of certain souls. In the lines which follow there is question of her Director. Jesus said to her on July 28:—"Your hearts are like waters from the same source which in the beginning take a separate way, but unite at length to form a larger stream, which is much more advantageous. They are like two stems of lilies a little distant from each other; as they grow they intermingle their flowers and their immaculate whiteness and sweet perfume rejoice the Heart of God. You, like these lilies, beloved souls of My holy Minister and my faithful servant, are so united to My Heart by Its loving embraces, that you are to receive the mission of making It known and loved more and more. The way is open to you but it is indeed thorny and sown with obstacles."

We read on the 12th of August:—"Jesus compares my soul to a ball, which when thrown violently to the ground, rises much higher than its point of departure; so my soul humbled by aridity rises again, by the grace of God, to the practice of pure love. He constantly predicts to me new sufferings, and does not fear to frighten me, assuring me that Crosses are most precious caresses which He reserves for privileged-souls. He shows me the state of victim as a sublime state. At another time I heard from my Beloved a dolorous plaint. He revealed to me the sorrow of His Heart at being robbed of the love which is due to Him, while souls are making so bad a use of it everywhere. He compared Himself to a beggar who sees food thrown away and spoiled right before his eyes, food which would prevent him from dying of starvation."

On August 22, she pours out her soul in these words:—O how I love to think of the love Jesus bears me! And yet this sweet thought is a source of pain to me; if I abandon myself to joy in knowing that my good Master loves me with a special love, I deduce from it that I am obliged to correspond to this special love, and I feel incapable of doing so. I know, however, for He Himself has told me so, that He blends bitterness with all my joys so as to guard me from self-seeking in His divine consolations. Crushed under the weight of my misery and weakness, I supplicate Jesus to come to my assistance and give me a little fervor. To comfort me He answers that this state, instead of coming to an end, will be accentuated more and more because I have not yet reached the *summit* of sorrow, and that as soon as I shall have arrived there I shall mount rapidly to Him. I suffer because I do not know how to suffer; consequently I am afraid of offending Jesus, which prevents me from going to Him with perfect confidence. Jesus wishes that I should die to all things; I understand this very well, but I rebel at His work of Mercy and hence my suffering is prolonged."

Her Divine Master deigns again to comfort her:—"Courage, My spouse, take heart; thy God is always near although thou dost not always see or hear Him. Sentiment, while giving certitude, diminishes faith; I take away sensible consolation from the soul that I wish to exercise perfectly in this virtue. There is question of believing without seeing, of believing without understanding and without wishing to understand. Thus reason is subjected and the soul glorifies God. Dost thou wish to give Him pleasure? Do not scrutinize His designs in thy regard; let Him treat thee as He pleases. He can do in one minute, by a single act of His will a thing which would require many years of labor. I know thou dost love prayer much; but believest thou that in praying as long a time as thou desirest, and as is thy custom, thou dost satisfy fully the demands of duty? I, who see much more clearly than thyself, perceive in thy heart a gnawing worm. Its work does not appear outwardly; but I discover hidden in its depths a secret complacency, a refined pride which conceals itself under the appearance of piety, and leads thee to adopt practices which serve very often only to nourish thy self-love. What does the Divine Spouse do then? He strikes, He cuts off without pity, without compassion, without listening to the laments of poor wounded nature: I take away everything that is spoiled and corrupted so that the evil may not become greater."

On September 3, Jesus once again asked of this loving soul the gift of her whole being:—"I want thee to lend me thy mind, thy life, thy faculties, which are My gifts, that thou mayst become wholly the instrument of My Mercy. The desire of seeing My adorable Heart ever more known and loved ought to move thee to receive this mission with docility. Accept it, then, through the love thou hast for My Sacred Heart, and in order to fulfill it, enter into the Order of the Visitation."

This is the first time that Our Lord showed clearly to His future spouse the Institute He had chosen for her. After this announcement of His Will, He continues to invite, to press and solicit her to yield to His desires. "The Monastery will be the pulpit in which thou shalt make Me known. Having no need of strength, I shall lean upon thy weakness. I use the ignorant to confound the strong."

We read in her notes of October 23:—"Jesus asked me this morning if I loved Him. I answered that I wished to love Him. He asked me afterward if I was willing to do what He desired. On my response in the affirmative, He sent me to say to a soul as discouraged as myself: Have confidence, Jesus loves you. I confessed to Him my embarrassment, never having seen the person. He answered by pointing her out to me; This is she. I experienced a moment of hesitation as usual, but my sweet Master reassured me, adding that I ought to obey without fearing that the inspiration might come from the enemy, it being entirely opposed to his plot, for he was trying to cause the loss of this soul by distrust."

Maria Consolata obeyed. Then the devil avenged himself by plunging her once more into her habitual fears—of self-illusion and deception of others. Her soul was enveloped in darkness; and while she consoled and enlightened so many other souls, even that of her Guide, she herself remained languid and tormented by frightful phantoms.

On November 8, 1903, she writes:—"My Jesus wishes that I should make the vow of humility, which consists, he told me, in recognizing that I am nothing without the aid of God, and in desiring to be unknown and despised. He told me to execute without delay or hesitation all that He had asked of me." And on December 28: —"I am confused but ravished with the cares my Beloved lavishes upon me. It is now more than a year since I began to write in obedience; and my Divine Master assures me that I shall never be discovered; there was danger of it several times, but His goodness did not permit it. He deigns to warn me when I must stop writing; and at other times when I deem it prudent to interrupt my work, He says to me: Thou mayst continue!"

We see in her notes of January 1, 1904, that the dear child continues in the same state of aridity:"I feel a violent disgust for all things; I am displeased with everything. I can find no relief in God, because I no longer feel His Presence, nor in creatures because they must not know my sufferings. I know not on what side to turn; but I conclude there is nothing to be done but to await with resignation the hour of deliverance. At times I ask myself anxiously if it is not indiscreet zeal on my part to write notes and bear messages to persons whom I am so slightly acquainted with. However, I shall not oppose the designs of God over me; I consent willingly, in spite of my repugnance, to surrender myself into His Divine hands as a simple instrument. Let Him use me as He pleases; I am His possession; let Him spare me in nothing and for nothing."

And on the 21st:—"This evening I experienced such violent spiritual pain that a special grace was necessary to enable me to endure it. I can explain neither the kind of pain nor the cause of it; I felt a great isolation of heart, and my will was grievously afflicted by nature; but with the grace of God I did not yield, and I relapsed into my state of aridity. To prove my love for Our Lord I shall satisfy my nature in nothing; even in the most pressing necessities, though it should tremble and revolt, I will that Love should triumph, Live Jesus, who desires that I shoud die in Him and for Him!"

On the 29th of the same month we read:—"Jesus has renewed today the promise He formerly made me of granting me great graces; and what consoled me above all was that He said creatures would recognize in me the effects of fidelity to grace, and that by this means I shall gain to His Heart many faithful souls."

She writes on February 3:—"While preparing for my devotion of the Wednesdays in honor of St. Joseph, Jesus told me that I would do well to deprive myself of drink on that day; not having permission for it today, He invites me to perform two mortifications among those which cost me most." Some days afterward Maria Consolata heard these words:—"Act in such a way that wherever the body can find relief, it may meet, on the contrary, only constraint and suffering; refuse it even the least pleasure."

On March 9, 1904, she speaks of her happiness at the thought of being able ere long to realize her ardent desires for the religious life:—"Time is passing, and I see the happy day approaching when I shall bid farewell to the world and go to bury myself in the beloved sepulchre of the Heart of Jesus; there one lives to die and dies to live. I need a life of continual obedience; I feel that obedience alone can maintain peace of conscience." On the 26th Maria Consolata experienced a desire to visit one of her cousins, a Religious of the Visitation of Turin: but Our Lord required this sacrifice of her, as he would despoil her of every satisfaction too eagerly sought.

On the 3rd of July, Jesus awakened her as usual at four in the morning, and said to her:—"Listen, My Joy, thou sleepest well on the Heart of thy Spouse; do not give so much care to thy body; habituate thyself to a life of sacrifice and refuse energetically all that it demands. Thou must conquer or die! If thou wilt practice mortification faithfully, thou wilt come to feel no longer the corporal necessities, which will be an excellent thing; for then thou canst remain in constant union with God, the Sovereign Good of thy soul."

Nothing could be more touching than the goodness which the Divine Master displays toward her. Now He encourages her to continue writing, telling her that she shall not be surprised; again He counsels her not to begin her work, as she will be immediately interrupted; He even goes so far as to tell her to take her walk without an umbrella under a dark and threatening sky, assuring her that it will not rain, etc., etc.

On August 31, 1904, the Divine Lover comes to ask her love. Like a mendicant He stands at the door of the hearts of His creatures and knocks. He complains sadly and tenderly to our dear Sister of their coldness:—"Behold. I beg the love of My creatures, who refuse it to Me and squander it upon things which pass away. They do not even think of giving it to Me. If thou knewest, Maria, how painful it is to love so much and not to be loved! I do not grow weary, I am always seeking love and no one gives it to me; not only they will not love Me, but they hate Me. Dost thou know what hinders Me from striking sinners? It is the prayers of the just; they disarm My divine Justice." And on the 15th of September:—"Thou canst not imagine, O my spouse, the pleasure I experience in remaining with My creatures! I am always in search of hearts that love Me, and I find only a small number. I lavish upon them the plenitude of My graces; I have so great a love for the souls who are faithful to Me and let Me do what I please with them, that I am as ready to gratify them as if it were a law to Me."

The Adorable Master complains anew on October 17, 1904, to His little Benjamin:—"The wicked triumph; few souls remain faithful; they abandon Me to seek for happiness where it is not to be found. O My spouse, can they be happy while violating a law so holy, so good and easy as Mine?"

Her Divine Spouse often speaks to her of her religious vocation. He reiterates His desire that she should enter the Visitation, promising her a more fatherly and loving assistance, greater graces, and communications more intimate when she shall be wholly His own:—"I invite thee to come to Me," He says, "because I wish thee to be all Mine; I am satisfied that thou shouldst go to the Visitation. Thou wilt soon be there and thou wilt be My consolation. My spouse, if thou knewest the desire I have of seeing thee all My own!" And two days afterward:—"My invitations and solicitations are pressing, because I desire so ardently that thou shouldst go to the Visitation. While waiting, read attentively the book of the Rules, and when thou shalt have studied it profoundly, I will conduct thee there."

On September 30, our future Sister asked Jesus with childlike frankness: "How was it that yesterday, before leaving the Church through obedience, I felt so much anguish?"-"It was a foretaste," He replied, "of what thou shalt suffer when thou shalt be wholly united with Me, filled with Me." Our dear Sister continued with enchanting candor to impart to Him her feelings: "I am grieved," she says, "at seeing that I derived such pleasure from a gift of grapes, and yet I do not experience so much when I receive My Jesus." He answered with infinite goodness :-"But this is nothing; it is common to all creatures: through duty thou lovest Me above all things; but thou dost experience more sensibility for natural things."

Our Lord referred anew to the Monastery on October 12, 1904:

"Thou shalt go to the Visitation," He said, "1. Because it is My Will; 2. Because at the Visitation thou canst not only become holy, but thou canst attain to the degree of sublime perfection which I destine for thee; 3. For the spiritual good of others. Follow the Rule, but without fear, for it is wholly impregnated with love and mercy. Thinkest thou that when thou shalt be all Mine, My Heart will cease to be for thee an Asylum of Mercy, as it has been heretofore? O My spouse, My beloved, I will recompense bountifully thy sacrifices and renunciations." And on October 23:—"When thou shalt have tasted the life of the cloister thou wilt not desire to return to the world at any cost. There thou wilt find humiliation, recollection, and all that is needful for thee. I will have My profit when thou art in the Monastery, for thou shalt win souls to Me. I desire ardently that thou shouldst be all Mine; at present creatures still have rights over thee."

On March 12, 1905, He said to her:—"Learn for thine own benefit and teach it to others, that to obtain solid virtue it must be sought in the Heart of Jesus. Whoever wishes to be saved has only to take refuge in this Blessed Ark whence he can look out upon the tempest without being shaken by its fury. O beloved spouse, discover to all the place of refuge thou hast chosen for thy perpetual Abode; do Me this charity to teach it to other souls that they may come and find Me. I have immense treasures of grace for all: and whoever comes to Me shall be overwhelmed with them."

He says on the 15th of the same month:—"Knowest thou the shortest way to arrive at Heaven? It is that of confidence in My merits and fidelity to grace." And on the 17th:—"My beloved, seek for Me Victims who are willing to immolate themselves for the glory of My Heart. My Heart is full of mercy, not only for thee, but for all."

It is to be regretted that we cannot give more at length these writings, marked with divine delicacy and sweetness. They are torrents of infinite tenderness, springing from the Heart of our Spouse; they are full of encouragement, sweet and urgent at the same time; of teachings clear and practical, phrased with admirable simplicity; they are words of consolation, but of a consolation at once strong and delicious. It is the supernatural, the divine, which attracts the soul to irresistible transports of confidence and love!

Some resolutions and reflections of Maria Consolata will impress upon us still more the delicate attention and minute detail to which

her fidelity was carried. They were written during the course of a
little retreat she made in the Autumn of 1905:—"I will have only
one single ambition," she declares, "to belong to Jesus forever.
I resolve to give Him every day new proofs of love. Thanks to
God, it seems to me I have no extraordinary attachment to the
things of the world. I love automobiles; but if I had to choose
between the riches of those who possess automobiles and the poverty
of Jesus Christ, I would prefer to be a beggar for His love.—However I am taken up with many things, while I ought only to think
of God. How many persons there are of whom I often think, and
whom I love tenderly! Can I say therefore that I love my God?
Is it not an act of propriety to dispose of a heart which no longer
belongs to me?—I notice that my will always wants to prevail over
that of others; it seems to me that there is no good but that which I
do.—It costs me to yield and I cannot resolve to do so easily. O
this wonderful *I*, how living it is!—When I succeed in anything, I
am eager to teach it to others, that they, too, may have the pleasure
of succeeding. I must absolutely watch over my heart, since for
the love of Jesus, I shall soon forsake creatures. When I am in the
Monastery my heart must not be filled with the things I have left.—
I must change my life and give up everything. The elastic ribbon
with which I close my books, seems to me an object of luxury;
I will dispense with it.—I take too much pleasure in the enjoyment
of good health and I grow sad when I am fatigued.—I do not like
to wear old shoes, my self-love is pained.—I often look into the
mirror; this I can easily avoid. Yes, for the love of Jesus I shall
mortify my senses, and do just the opposite of what self-love suggests.—I allow myself to pet a dog, but I shall do so no longer, for
my heart belongs entirely to Jesus.—When I undertake any labor,
I trust too much in myself; and when it is finished, I am eager to
show that I have succeeded in the affair; this also is pride.—Well,
from today I shall manage things so that nothing I do shall be admired or esteemed, and thus give a good lesson to my proud nature.
I will suffer joyously since Jesus wills it; I will not seek calm and
tranquillity, but let Jesus do around me whatever He pleases. I shall
be faithful to the practice of virtue, even in the smallest things;
for example, I shall be silent when I wish to speak, and speak when
I would like to keep silence. May Jesus bless me, guide me, and
enlighten me!"

The Divine Master continues to entertain Himself familiarly

with her: every day He speaks to her, exciting and encouraging her to enter the Monastery:—"To be a Visitandine," He said to her on January 6, 1906, "means to enjoy the special glory which the Order of the Visitation will have in Heaven for having propagated the devotion to My Sacred Heart. Although all in the Communities do not cooperate directly, yet all participate in the same glory, as members of the Order."

O yes! the Adorable Master is benignly tender and loving with His little spouse. But we must desist, for it is impossible to abridge the divine colloquies. It would rob them of their sweetness, their freshness, and their celestial fragrance. It is impossible also to follow in its minute details the wonderful work that Jesus operated in this faithful soul.

III

IN THE HOLY ARK: POSTU-
LANT, NOVICE, PROFESSED
NUN

Maria Consolata sighed ardently after the cloister. Entirely surrendered to her God and possessed by Him, she practiced a mortification austere and intense in order to destroy her nature. Being
called to a profound interior life, she felt the need of a silent and hidden Nest. Her parents yielded at last to her desires; but it is easy to
imagine how heart-rending was their sacrifice. They conducted her at
first to the Monastery of Pozzo Strada; but not receiving a favor-
able answer, they addressed the Sisters of Pignerol, where Maria
Consolata, after having made a little retreat, was accepted in March,
1906, and admitted to her trial.

From the moment of her entrance into the Holy Ark, the dear
dove was penetrated with the atmosphere one breathes there. Was
not this just what she had sought? Nothing could suit her better
than this cloistered life; to be so near her God, free to converse
with Him, delivered from the daily solicitudes of the household,
what happiness! But there also Jesus was awaiting her; He so good,
so tender, so condescending to her, was again preparing a bitter
chalice.

Maria, in the enthusiasm of her joy, opened her heart with the
candor of a child to the Superior then in charge: she imparted to
her some of the divine communications, her transports of love,
and her vehement desire to attain a sublime degree of perfection.
The venerable Mother, deeply impressed by such revelations, astonished to find in a soul so young such riches of grace, such exceptional gifts, to hear her speak even of an extraordinary mission she
had to fulfill, asked herself if in accepting this Postulant she was not
acting contrary to the intentions of our Holy Founders, who rec-
ommend nothing to us so much as the spirit of simplicity, the dis-
tinctive mark of our Order.

Now it happened that while the venerated Mother of Pignerol was still in a state of indecision, our young Postulant was taken with a slight indisposition. This was at once made a pretext to restore her to her family; thus painful explanations were avoided; and her relatives were overjoyed at the final determination. Maria obeyed without a word. But who could reveal her martyrdom? Her heart was crushed. She repressed silently her bitter tears. Was this blessed Cloister, the object of her sighs, to be forever closed against her? Yet had not Jesus told her a thousand times He wished her to be a Visitandine? The fear of illusion, of having deceived herself and others, returned to torture her; and the enemy on his side tormented her incessantly, laying snares upon snares for her.

Wholly abandoned to the Will of God, no complaint escaped her; she put her lips to the painful chalice and absorbed all its bitter ness. Ever laborious and docile, she returned to her life of de votedness in the family, her heart broken but her countenance calm and sweet. She tried to dissemble her sufferings so as not to afflict her parents; in spite of her extraordinary self-control, tears often shone in her eyes, and fell silently; she knew how to eat the bread of sorrow with resignation, steeped in faith and confidence. One powerful thought sustained her and gave her courage: "Jesus will not abandon Me!"

Of this time of sorrow we have not a word or writing: there are certain deep agonies that have no word; there is a limit, which passed, all is veiled and hidden between the soul and God.

Weeks and months glided away. Maria turned to the sweet St. Francis de Sales, begging him to put an end to her long suspense; would he, a fountain of compassion for all, not have pity on her who sighed after the happiness of being his daughter?

In spite of her efforts to hide her anguish of soul, the poor child did not succeed. Her pale face and emaciated frame made known her great sorrow and her consuming desire of a blessing she could not obtain. Her parents perceived that their beloved daughter was failing daily, and they understood the cause. A great conflict was going on in their hearts; it was more violent in the heart of the venerable father, who declared that he would rather die than be separated from his dear treasure. But at last his religious sentiments triumphed over his tender natural affection, and he gave his consent for the second time. He imitated the faith of the patriarch Abraham, and sought himself the altar on which he was to immolate his child of predilection.

For our happiness it was to our Monastery of Como he applied. Our Lord told her interiorly that the Visitation of Como was the hollow place in the wall, the nest of the dove, where He willed her to be. Now she was ignorant even of the existence of the Visitation in that city. Such were the ways of Providence over this soul, and the hidden and admirable designs by means of which Jesus introduced her into the "place of her repose." The Most Honored Mother Maria Louisa Sobrero, whom our dear Turin with incomparable kindness had lent us, was then Superior. She knew the Ferrero family and held them in high esteem. Having made inquiries at Pignerol as to the dismissal of Maria Consolata from that Monastery, and having been apprized that the only obstacle to her admission was the extraordinary way by which she seemed to be led, Mother Maria Louisa hastened to open her arms and her heart to the dear aspirant.

In the meantime Maria had been counselled as her case, so uncommon, required; the lesson received at Pignerol was to warn her for the future. Of a nature simple, candid and open, she felt that prudential measure as a burden, but made the sacrifice; by her great obedience she obtained strength to bear in silence through long years the new and profoundly interior martyrdom which God, through the mouth of her Ecclesiastical Superiors, had imposed upon her.

Maria Consolata arrived among us on December 30, 1907, accompanied by her venerable father and her dear aunt; she was then twenty-two years old. Matured, purified by suffering, enriched by the virtues she had so long practiced in the shadow of the Cross, she seemed already formed to the religious life.

We admired her profound humility, her perfect obedience, her faithful fidelity, her habitual recollection. There was something noble and gracious in her words and actions that attracted all hearts: hence she was soon admitted to her trial.

The venerated Mother Maria Louisa, who was also Mistress of Novices, discovering in our dear Postulant extraordinary gifts, quickly appreciated the value of this soul and the acquisition made by the Community. But to prevent pride from spoiling the divine work, she resolved to form her to strong and solid virtue, and to spare her neither corrections nor humiliations. Sister Maria cor-

responded eagerly to her maternal cares, and we may say she was
far more avid to receive trials and reprimands than her good Mistress was to furnish them.

Our dear Sister carried fidelity to excess, we may say even to
scrupulosity; this often caused her to be perplexed and undecided, so
desirous she was of doing what was most perfect. She had a special power of introspection, and scrutinized with great minuteness
the least of her actions, her aim being to do all purely for God,—
an imperfection calculated to constrain the mind and subject it to
a painful and continual tension. Her prudent Mistress strenuous-
ly combated this natural tendency, urging the young Sister to act
contrary to it and thus acquire the liberty of spirit so necessary in
the spiritual life. Maria had a tenacious will and it cost her to yield
and surrender her judgment. This was her greatest battle-field. But
her silent struggles were crowned with success; and Jesus continued to replenish the soul of His beloved with His graces.

The Community, edified at the virtues of the Postulant, seeing
her so fervent and at the same time so humble, regarded her as a
treasure. Nevertheless no one suspected that we had in our midst
a new Ark of Alliance, guarding jealously the celestial manna· In
approaching or conversing with her, we were penetrated, attracted
by the supernatural which surrounded her; she truly radiated Jesus·
Her eyes were ordinarily lowered; if she raised them toward Heaven
or spoke of her Beloved, they appeared beautiful and luminous; one
could read in them the virginal purity of her soul and the divine
love which devoured her. She always spoke sweetly, peacefully;
and we learn from her precious writings that she never said a word
without having consulted her Divine Master. We could not doubt
that nature, entirely conquered, had yielded to grace.

Our dear Sister was gifted with perfect equality of humor; nothing could trouble her. She remained calm and serene amid the great
est difficulties, which led to the belief that she was naturally of a
cold and indifferent temperament; in reality, however, she had
acquired this evenness of temper by her constant fidelity in seconding
all the movements of grace; for she had a most sensitive, delicate
and affectionate heart, but creatures could not satisfy it. Hence,
plunged in continual recollection, despising all that could withdraw
her from God, she saw only Him, tended only to Him, and listened
only to Him.

In the progress of our recital we shall have occasion to speak of her fidelity to the least desires of obedience. We may be permitted to cite here an incident related of her while yet a postulant. A present had been made to our Monastery of a turtle, which had chosen a little corner of our garden for its home. One day our Honored Mother not seeing the turtle take its usual walk in the sun, invited the Sisters who were present to go and look for it; all obeyed but soon returned saying it could not be found. The young Postulant alone persisted in the hunt. "My Jesus," she said, "obedience works miracles; help me to do our Mother's will." Her fidelity was rewarded, and soon the dear Postulant came to us from the ex tremity of the garden with the turtle.

We shall pass rapidly over the time of her trial, having before us so vast a field; and content ourselves with saying that our dear Sister labored energetically to acquire solid virtues, casting the foundations sure and deep in order to build securely her spiritual edifice, destined to rise to so sublime a height.

After eleven months of fervor as a Postulant, Sister Maria, to the general satisfaction, was admitted to the Habit. Her happiness was indescribable; she could not find words to express her gratitude to her venerated Mother and Mistress. She prepared for the great act with angelic fervor; and on November 5, 1908, we saw her radiant under her white veil. Msgr. Carughi, Canon and Vicar General of our Diocese, performed the ceremony; and our dear Novice received the name of Sister Benigna Consolata. Her own name of Consolata was left her because it harmonized so well with the meekness of her character; for the same reason that of Benigna was combined with it, and also because November 5 was the anniversary of the death of Sister Jeanne Benigne Gojos. Our Honored Mother Maria-Louisa in giving her this name, seemed to enter into the designs of God since there was to be more than one trait of resemblance between these two privilegd souls.

In his sermon on the occasion Msgr. Carughi developed these words of St. Paul: *Vos estis Templum Dei Vivi.* He urged the happy Novice to form in herself a Holy Temple, a living Tabernacle for her God, following in this the example of our Holy Church, which converts a material edifice into the House of the Lord.

During her Novitiate our dear Sister was ever more and more exact in the observances, faithful to her duty, preventing toward the Sisters, knowing how to renounce her own desires in order to give them pleasure, most prompt, above all, in humbling herself profound ly, on every occasion. Consequently the Community admitted her to the Profession of the simple Vows at the end of her year. The ceremony was fixed for November 23, 1909. It was for our happy Sister the day she had so long desired and the most beautiful of her life, since it united her to her Jesus by indissoluble bonds. Her joy was indeed at its height. Msgr. Abbondio Ballerini, Director of the Seminary, then our Spiritual Father, presided over the ceremony; and, as on the day of the Clothing, the sermon was preached by Msgr. Carughi, who, inspired from on High, pointed out to our newly Professed Sister the way in which she should walk. He summarized his discourse in these three words; Faith, Love, Sacrifice.

We who have had the happiness of living with our angelic Sister, can affirm with truth that she fully realized the program traced out for her that blessed day. We find no note which might reveal to us the impressions of Sister Benigna Consolata on the day of her profession. Perhaps the Sacred Spouse had pressed her to His Heart in silence with infinite tenderness; again, perhaps she preferred to keep jealously the treasures of love He had lavished upon her, the better to say: *Secretum meum mihi.*

Our Most Honored Mother Maria-Louisa Sobrero, in the beginning of her second triennial, 1910, relinquished her charge of Mistress of Novices, which she conferred on our dear Sister Josephine Antoinette Scazziga, at present (1919) our beloved Mother.

The new Mistress discerned at once that our dear Sister was an elect soul, called to extraordinary sanctity. In the meantime, while admiring her rare virtues, she noticed that her spirit was not free, in consequence of unfounded fears which paralyzed the action of grace, and prevented her from advancing rapidly in the way of our holy vocation. She always appeared tranquil, calm and smiling; but the able Mistress perceived that she did not enjoy that perfect peace which is the portion of faithful souls. When Sister Benigna Consolata disclosed to her some of her dispositions (without however unveiling her secret) her affectionate and prudent Mistress compared her soul to a little barque fastened to the bank, or to a bird which cannot fly because it is held by a thread, or again, to a poor little lamb caught in a thicket. Our dear Sister was then suffering a cruel martyrdom. She would have been glad to pour out her soul with that candor and simplicity which bring us happiness and repose, but this was not permitted by her Directors. We shall see later how it was given her to open her heart entirely to her Superior, and how this disclosure became a new source of graces in reward for the interior sufferings of which her long silence had been the cause.

Meanwhile Jesus prepared a new Cross for His beloved. On February 26, 1912, a telegram brought the news of the unexpected death of Signora Ferrero. She had just written to her dear daughter, terminating her letter with the words: "I leave you in the Heart of Jesus." Our Most Honored Mother communicated the sad news as gently as possible to our dear Sister. "When she returned to the wardrobe," says the Sister who was her aid, "her face was flooded with tears; she tried to write to her family, but she could not succeed, her heart was so crushed with grief. Suddenly, taking her crucifix, she kissed it, pressed it to her heart, and watered it with her tears. Then, consoled and fortified, she set to work to write holy and affectionate lines, full of comfort, to her afflicted family."

"O how can anyone say that the Monastery is the tomb of the affections! " she said afterward. "If the Lord, when there is question of corresponding to His call, gives us strength to break the ties He Himself has created, the religious life not only does not require us to forget those whom we love, but rather increases supernaturally our affection; it ennobles and divinises it." The letters which she wrote to her relatives were overflowing with religious tenderness; she forgot no one; she had cordial expressions of sympathy for each, even for the domestics, to whom she sent kind messages with little souvenirs and pictures.

Sister Benigna Consolata, being gifted with a solid judgment, a healthy mind, and a kind heart, was extremely useful to our Community. She had a special aptitude for mathematics; and several books in the Monastery contain numerous pages of her beautiful writings.

Thanks to some lessons received from her brother, who was an engineer, our dear Sister succeeded in placing several electric wires in the Monastery, taking upon herself also to make the necessary reparations. She had charge of the gas fixtures: one evening the gas refused to give light in the Assembly Room; after having tried by all possible means to light it, Sister Benigna Consolata took the fixture apart, and having unscrewed the little tube, she saw that a spider web hindered the free passage of the gas. Our beloved Sister, who drew a supernatural lesson from everything, suddenly exclaimed; "O what a lesson this spider gives us! A little nothing is sufficient to arrest the operations of grace in our souls."

Her perfect fidelity in corresponding to the least inspirations of grace revealed to her by experience that nothing can more surely attract Jesus and hold Him in the soul than this faithful fidelity at every instant. One day—it was during the morning recreation— the Community was at work in a little grove of nut-trees, and the sun, striking through the branches, incommoded our Sisters. "The branches and leaves do not suffice to shelter us from these burning rays," said our Honored Mother. "We ought to have a tent here." All had understood; but our fervent Sister Benigna Consolata alone took her work and disappeared to seek some means of satisfying the maternal desire. After a moment of absence she returned bearing, for want of something better, some yards of linen crash which she stretched among the branches. The expedient met with imperfect success, but our Sister had obeyed. Another time—it was a winter evening during recreation— Sister Benigna Consolata approaching our Mother said to her: "My Mother, if Your Charity will permit, I will go and close the windows of the room where we extend the linen; they are still open." "But how do you know they are still open?" "My Mother," our dear Sister answered humbly, "since Your Charity told us in the summer that it would be prudent to notice before night if those windows were closed, I have gone there every evening." (It is to be noted that these windows overlooked a little poultry-yard, and could not be seen except from the room itself.) Our venerated Mother was as consoled as edified by this perfect fidelity in the beginning of a religious life.

It was with great joy and feelings of profound gratitude toward God that our Honored Mother presented the little Benjamin of Jesus at the altar on the day of her Solemn Profession. It took place on November 12, 1912. We shall not speak of the happiness of the dear Novice: only those souls called to taste these ineffable delights are capable of understanding their sweetness.

The second triennial of our beloved Mother Maria Louisa Sobrero being terminated, the Lord placed us, at the Ascension of 1913, under the blessed government of our incomparable Mother Josephine Antoinette Scazziga. Shortly after, our venerated Sister Déposée was recalled by our Monastery of Turin, where she was elected Superior. We shall not attempt to paint the mournful scene of separation: we have already spoken of it in our little Circular. Sister Benigna Consolata was deeply affected at her departure, for very special bonds united her to our venerated Mother; and many of the Sisters looked upon her with admiration controlling her emotions so generously, that she did not shed a tear nor yield to any natural weakness, as often happens with tender and affectionate hearts such as hers, but less mortified. Our fervent Sister, being at this time Second Procuratrix, helped courageously at the packing and other preparations for departure; the pallor of her face alone betrayed the violence of her efforts at self-command.

When God creates great souls He prepares for their guidance persons fitted to direct them in the way He Himself has already traced out. The Divine Master was the first Director of His Benjamin. "It is I who am thy Director," He said to her one day. And another time: "It is I who teach thee humility: it is I, too, who enable thee to discover the snares of the enemy." But desiring to use human means to accomplish His works, the Lord deigned to surround our dear Sister from the cradle to the tomb with holy and enlightened souls. She speaks of her first Director in the following terms:— "Among so many graces with which I have been favored, I must count that of having had an enlightened Spiritual Father, who having taken me under his direction when I was about twelve years old, never ceased until my entrance into religion, to counsel me, to enlighten my mind and fortify my heart. It is to him, after God, that I owe the happiness of being a Visitandine. While I was still enjoying our sweet family life at home, he placed in my hands the lives of our dear Sisters Ann Madeleine Remusat, (the Marguerite Marie of Marseilles), and Jeanne Benigne Gojos, (a saintly Sister of Turin favored with extraordinary graces), as well as other spiritual books fitted to set aglow in my heart the sacred fire which Jesus had enkindled there. The reading of these lives cast more deeply the roots of my vocation."

We think it opportune here to quote two letters from her Director, the Canon Boccardo. The first dated July 6, 1910, was addressed to her some months after her Profession of the simple Vows:—

My dear Daughter in the Heart of Jesus.

You have been surprised at my long silence and justly so. But what would you? Among other reasons, my first is that treating of the secrets of your conscience, I could not forward a letter without being *absolutely certain* that my writing should not pass through the hands of another. You can very well confer with the Father of your soul, since he alone is capable of understanding fully your state.

For several days something that I read in the life of the Venerable John Vianny [1] has been running through my mind, and I think it will be excellent for you. The Saint possessed the secret of concentrating himself upon the present action which he was doing, without adverting to the action he had just finished or to that which he was to do afterwards. It is the theory and practice of your (and also my) St. Francis de Sales; "Let your mind pass sweetly," he said, "from one action to another, without *eagerness* or disquietude."

Does Sister Benigna act thus? It is a deceit of the evil one that makes us act otherwise; to be disquieted lest the preceding action, whatever it be, has been badly performed, argues a motive of fear. And although it is a deceit yet it will prevent actions still before us from being taken in hand. Thus while you are thinking of the past you spoil the present; and you spoil it also by foreseeing the subsequent one, which for the moment is an intruder. Leave the past to the mercy of God—little by little it passes—and abandon the future to His Paternal Providence. We have at our disposal only the present. Set aside forever all these minute investigations of whatever kind.............Delicacy of conscience leads to a more perfect love of your Spouse, but scrupulosity is a disease. Now, delicacy is not afflicted, not even at the least things, it being always understood that in this life whatever care we take, our works will always bear the mark of the manufactory, that is, of imperfection. But leave to Jesus Himself the grateful office of being *the repairer of our defects*, as He told the Blessed Alacoque, [2] and no longer meddle with them If you do otherwise, without your perceiving it, you will be lost in continual self-scrutiny and self-satisfaction, which will weaken your mind and hinder the mysterious and loving operations of Jesus in your soul. I bless you with all my heart.

1.—The Curé of Ars, born at Lyons, France, May 8, 1786, died at Ars, August 4, 1859. Proclaimed Blessed by Pius X in 1905.
2.—Saint Margaret Mary Alacoque, the Apostle of the Sacred Heart, 1647-1690, canonized by Benedict XV, May 13, 1920.

The second letter is dated August 21, 1912, some months previous to her Solemn Profession:—

My dear Daughter in the Sacred Heart of Jesus,

Your simplicity not only does not astonish me but it pleases me greatly. I am not surprised to learn that you are in the Monastery as a statue in its niche. I knew very well that the Visitation was made for you and you for it; but to hear you say so increases my happiness; with you and for you I bless our Jesus. I know nothing better to say to you than these words of David:-*Specie tua et pulchritudine tua, intende, prospere, procede, et regna."*[1] Advance in the beautiful way of love if you wish to attain the end of your vocation: and hence you must forsake yourself in order to please Him who despoiled Himself of His infinite Majesty for love of us, real nothings. Do not fear to be wanting in respect to Him when you act familiarly with Him: it makes Him so happy! O yes, be content to be the little grain of sand carried away by the dust of the road. As to the rules I gave you on the part of Jesus, put them in practice constantly; I am responsible for them. You have always been *mother of fear;* you are so still; I read it between your lines. Remember that if the fear of God is necessary, it is nevertheless only the *beginning of wisdom;* [2] it is not the salt we put into the soup which nourishes us, but the soup itself. Live in love and confidence with Jesus; this is much better. Perfect charity casteth out fear. [3]

Msgr. Alfonso Archi, Bishop of Como, was the principal Director of this chosen soul after her entrance among us. Sister Benigna Consolata held his Lordship in profound respect and gave him her entire confidence. On his side our saintly Prelate regarded the young religious, so modest and humble, with the highest esteem and consideration. During her last illness he gave her every mark of his fatherly devotedness; and he deigns to continue it by favoring the diffusion of her writings. We shall cite one of the letters his Lordship addressed to her from time to time to tranquillize and encourage her:—

1.—Ps. XLIV. 5.   2.—Ecclus. I. 16.   3.—I John, IV. 18.

Reverend Sister Benigna and dear Daughter in Jesus Christ:-

1. *I speak the truth in Jesus Christ, I lie not, my conscience bearing me witness in the Holy Ghost.* (St. Paul to the Romans, IX, 1) Unhappy I if I lie!

This then is the pure truth which ought to tranquillize you fully; the Christian soul and still more the religious soul, as far as lies in her power, copies the Divine Exemplar that she may become one thing with Him. He has paid for our sins, and the religious soul ought to unite with Him in expiation for herself and others, *purgationem peccatorum faciens.* Sister Benigna has done this and continues to do so. Now the said Sister Benigna *sits in an elevated place at the right hand of the divine complacencies* (St. Paul to the Hebrews, 1). O this ought to humiliate you profoundly! But if our Lord is glorified by humility, He is also glorified by the truth; hence, I repeat to you, *the divine pardon for your sins is certain and assured.*

2. And to excite you to love, cast your eyes on the Adorable Face of Jesus; on that divine brow which is the brightness, the splendor of Heaven, and which for the sins of the world, has veiled its glory,—*et tenebrae factae sunt*—on those Eyes which are the delight of Paradise, and are now filled with tears and blood; on that adorable Mouth, become mute, that Mouth which with a single *fiat* created the world out of nothing; on that Countenance, resplendent with beauty, now pale, livid, and disfigured.

3. To correspond with love to the graces received from Love, repeat with fervor the inflamed words of St. Paul:—*Who then shall separate us from the love of Christ? Shall tribulation, or distress, or famine, or nakedness, or danger, or persecution, or the sword? But in all these things we overcome because of him that hath loved us. ...For I am sure that neither death, nor life, nor Angels, nor principalities, nor powers, nor things present, nor things to come, nor might, nor height, nor depth, nor any other creature shall be able to separate us from the love of God, which is in Christ Jesus Our Lord."* (*Romans*, ch. VIII.) Therefore, *I am crucified to the world and the world is crucified to me.* (Galatians, ch. VI.) "*I live no longer, but Christ liveth in me. ...My love makes me live for Him who so loved me as to deliver Himself for me.* (Gal. ch. II.) And I bless you!

Como, April 26, 1916.   ALFONSO, BISHOP.

Our venerated Spiritual Father, Msgr. Catelli, also directed our Sister with prudence and wisdom, qualities highly appreciated by the souls who have the happiness to be under his direction.

Lastly, the Canon Piccinelli, Confessor of the Community, was "the visible angel" who sustained and guided her more intimately during her religious life with paternal devotedness. We will not pause here to eulogize this holy priest, for whatever we might say would fall far below the reality: we will only observe that Our Lord deigned to show Sister Benigna Consolata how dear he was to His Heart. Several times while he was celebrating Holy Mass or giving Benediction, she saw the Divine Infant Jesus clinging to his neck and bestowing upon him a thousand caresses. Our dear Sister learned from her good Master that he had attracted these extraordinary favors by his profound humility. We will not say more, fearing to wound the modesty of our venerated Confessor; however, we must add that he has justly acquired the esteem and gratitude of our Community.

Our Most Honored Mother perceived at once that if she would fully cooperate with the divine designs over the soul of our dear Sister, she must guard her with maternal vigilance. Humility must be rooted more and more in her soul; therefore she must be surrounded with humiliation as a protecting hedge. Our Mother was naturally sweet and mild and not led to make corrections; she confessed to us that during the first months of her Superiority, she had prayed Our Lord to give her strength to reprove in public as well as in private, as our holy Rule prescribes. Her Charity said simply to several of us that it caused her real suffering to give a reprimand; but when there was question of Sister Benigna Consolata, He gave her a special grace, for she humbled her severely and fearlessly.

On one occasion, our dear Sister being then assistant to the Novitiate, she gave a little commission to the novices without telling the Mistress beforehand. The thing was so trifling that had there been question of another no notice would have been taken of it; but our Honored Mother, who let nothing pass in her virtuous daughter, had her advertised in the refectory. In presence of the Community she reproved her severely, telling her that she ought not to pretend to become Mistress of Novices and Superior, that her place was the last and she ought to remain hidden, dispensing herself from commanding the novices as if she were their Mistress, etc. Our venerated Mother went so far as to repeat to her several times in Chapter the same words, so hard to self-love.

Our beloved Sister who wished to do all things perfectly, applied herself with earnestness to her labors, but worked slowly. She was often reproached with this, occasion being taken to mortify her. She received the correction on her knees and humbled herself sin_cerely. Her interior conflict was revealed by the blush which covered her face for an instant; but it passed and our dear Sister resumed her calm and serene air.

She received with no less humility the abjection which came upon her at times in consequence of her long spiritual conferences. When these were prolonged beyond the dinner of the second table [1] our Sisters in charge of the Refectory and Dispensary had to lose the recreation in order to attend upon the poor late-comer, who would have preferred to eat dry bread rather than impose the least sacrifice upon others; but above all things she would be faithful to the Rule, and silencing her own sentiments to immolate them to duty, she took her repast gravely, as is prescribed. When she arrived in the Community room, in spite of her profoundly humbled air, we teased her immoderately. Our Mother herself, before she had become aware of the divine communications, used to say a few words in praise of the common life, which, setting aside all singularity, does not allow one to be too much occupied with self. Our humble Sister bent her head over her work not saying a word; if questioned, she answered with her ordinary sweetness, not betraying her inward struggle. Later, she spoke of the powerful self-control that was necessary over her desire to hasten from the Confessional and take her dinner quickly, in order to be sooner at the recreation. "No, I ought to act only for God," she said, "without considering what creatures will say or think; besides a little shame will be very good for me, who were it not for the divine mercy, would be precipitated into the most profound depths of hell. Cost what it will, then, I shall not hurry; no, all for Jesus and nothing for self."

We have already cited examples of her fidelity to obedience; here is another related by a Sister of the Novitiate. "One day," she tells us, "having gone with my Sister Benigna Consolata to the garden to gather the dry leaves, I observed that since there were so few, it would be a loss of time to carry them to the place assigned; but she answered with her ordinary sweetness:—My

---

[1]. About 11 A.M.: the Sisters dine at 10.

Sister, our Mother desires we should carry them there; we ought to obey although we had to pick up only a single leaf. I was greatly edified," adds the Sister, "and I saw that until then I had not understood obedience." We may remark that apart from the occupations of her employment, our dear Sister having much to write, economized her time as much as possible; this was for her a good act of mortification and self-denial.

To renounce oneself in this manner from time to time is good; but to let pass no occasion of self-sacrifice—this is the martyrdom of the will, a martyrdom no less meritorious in the eyes of God than that of blood. If the Divine Spouse was ravished by a single hair of the Spouse of the Canticles, with what love He must have accepted the continual immolations of His chosen soul!

In 1913, Sister Benigna Consolata was appointed Refectorian. Of a delicate constitution and subject to chills, she soon had an attack of rheumatism so acute and obstinate that several months were required to cure it, in spite of drastic remedies and the affectionate cares which were lavished upon her. Sweet and patient, our dear Sister was happy to embrace the Cross of her Jesus, happy in having a new occasion to prove to Him her love.

Notwithstanding her severe pains, always faithful to duty, she followed regularly the common life; but we divined her sufferings from the sudden contractions of her countenance; the crisis passed, she at once became calm and smiling, leaving us edified at her patience.

She was put in charge of the linen wardrobe some time after ward, and devoted herself with all her heart to her new employment; but there again her union with God rendered activity difficult. Re primands were the result, which she received sweetly, accusing herself even more and saying she deserved still greater reprehensions.

IV

HER HUMILITY, OBEDIENCE,

MORTIFICATION, CHARITY

We come to the close of the year 1914. Sister Benigna Consolata not having obtained permission of the Ecclesiastical Superiors, had not yet revealed the divine secret to her who represents Jesus to us here below. But we will let our Honored Mother speak:—
"O what a martyrdom our dear Sister had to suffer! She who possessed so fully the spirit of our Institute, and whose interior attraction was to tell all, to confide all to her Mother! But she could not do so without contravening obedience. Our venerated Ecclesiastical Superiors had imposed upon her a rigorous silence while they were examining her words and writings that they might be assured of the truth of the divine communications. When the Lord chose us for Mother of this little Community, He gave us at the same time a maternal tenderness for every one of the Sisters, and an ardent desire to make them advance in the perfection of divine love. Among the most fervent, Sister Benigna Consolata distinguished herself by her rapid progress in virtue; but we could not account for the doubts, the fears and uncertainties that tortured her soul; the dear child was for us an enigma.

"At last the day and hour came, and she was permitted to open the door of her mystic sanctuary; from that moment she entered into the way of perfect liberty of spirit, and torrents of peace and joy overflowed her soul, so that she could say with David— *I have run in the way of Thy commandments because Thou hast dilated my heart.*—We should never end if we were to attempt to sound the abyss of our dear Sister's humility. The remembrance of little faults, declared and detested a thousand times, kept her in a habitual state of compunction; she put herself below all the Sisters, esteeming them far better and more virtuous. One day she said with tears in her eyes:—'My Mother, when I see our Sisters so good, so virtuous, pure as angels, I look upon myself as an intruder. Do you know to what I compare myself? To that corner of the garden allotted to the sweepings of the house; a few bushes and even flowers hide them from the passers-by; as for myself', she added with enchanting simplicity, 'God has gifted me with a modest, grave and recollected exterior, to hide the defects of my soul. O if our Sisters knew me as I am!'

"Her humility, so sincere, was the more admirable since our Lord deigned to give her the most tender names: My Benigna, My Lily, My Dove, My Joy, My Benjamin, etc. The more He exalted her, the more she abased herself and plunged into the depth of her nothingness; the more He manifested her angelic virtue, the more avid she was of mortifications, humiliations, reiterated public advertisements, in order, she said, to ruin her self-love. She continually deplored in the bitterness of a contrite and humbled heart, what she called the disorders of her life, finding inexpressible sweetness in discovering her least natural movements, her evil inclinations, all those miseries, in a word, which are the sad heritage of our first parents. In her writings she speaks very often, through obedience, of her interior state; but more frequently still she assured us that she would have preferred to print her general confession than to publish the favors of which she was the object.

"Her contempt of self showed itself on every occasion. If advertisements were given in Community, Sister Benigna Consolata was promptly on her knees declaring her fault. If there was question of some infraction of the Rule, Sister Benigna Consolata accused herself in order to receive correction. Often she was innocent; we then reprehended her for the abuse she made of our holy practices, to make herself singular, we said. She would blush, being extremely sensitive to that kind of remark; but her ardent desire to resemble her Jesus led her to humiliate herself still more. And we profited adroitly," concludes our Honored Mother, "of the least occasion to try her virtue and maintain her in those excellent dispositions."

The Very Reverend Antonio Piccinelli, her Confessor, writes:-

"Docile to the divine instructions, Sister Benigna Consolata conformed in everything, as to the exterior, to the common life. But in her interior life all was extraordinary. Her humility was alarmed at this, and she entreated our Lord to diminish His favors in her regard. He then promised to withdraw them all rather than suffer a single flaw in that virtue so dear to His Heart. He assured her that He would hide them from the knowledge of others, allowing only her imperfections to appear; a very special favor among all the others."

Our dear Sister had a remarkable talent for painting. Among other beautiful works due to her pen and brush, we will mention a little Standard, representing St. Francis of Assisi sigmatized and in prayer, which she executed for the parish of Sottocornola. She wrote very well in round and in Gothic hand; knowing her kind heart and her sweet spirit of condescension, we often had recourse to her. When she was overburdened and could not gratify us immediately, she humbled herself, begging us to excuse her; and afterward hastened to comply with our desires. When the little task was finished, she would thank us for the pleasure we had given her in requesting the little service.

It was during the month which preceded the Superior's Feast that her precious assistance was most eagerly solicited. Her Charity had not a moment of leisure; and if she happened to be guilty of any forgetfulness, our Honored Mother spared neither correction nor advertisement, asking her what she did with her time. Sister Benigna Consolata would cast herself on her knees, accusing herself of slowness and dissipation; but for all that she did not cease to continue her good offices for us. However, with her habitual candor, she said sometimes to our Mother: "When I am so busy, and our Sisters come to ask a service of me, I am tempted to impatience, and would be glad to fly away from them:—but grace! O grace!" Yes, it was truly her fidelity to grace that most frequently brought upon her corrections, which she regarded as the most precious caresses of her Divine Spouse.

"My Benigna," He had said to her, "when a soul receives humiliations well, I give her a new mark of resemblance with Me. In telling thy faults, always choose those that humble thee the most; be a good treasurer for Heaven. To graft a plant the bark must be stripped off; this thou must do by mortification, in order that I, who am thy graft, may take life in thee."

Our Sister had not only a real contempt for herself, but she desired that everyone else should despise her; hence in telling her faults she used expressions that deeply impressed and edified us.

"My Benigna," Jesus said again to her, "the purity of love consists in the perfection of sacrifice; and there is no sacrifice which pleases me so much as that of one's honor and reputation. When a soul has attained to the love of contempt in order that God may be glorified in her, I look upon her with so much love that if she could see Me she would die of joy. But they fear contempt as they would fear a monster. Why is it that so many souls do not arrive at the summit of perfection? Because they are afraid of contempt. My Benigna, I have given thee a thirst for contempt, but I will increase it still more."

We shall tell ere long what a chalice of humiliation our dear Sister was destined to drink; and we shall see how great and strong was the love of this true spouse for her Beloved.

The last year of her life, having been appointed Assistant to the Novitiate, she asked and obtained the favor of telling her faults and performing all the accustomed practices like a little Novice. She was for us a great example of encouragement in receiving correction well. Her Divine Master had taught her on this subject:— "An advertisement well received may, during the time it lasts cause a soul to attain a union with Me which, perhaps, she could only have attained after two or three years of ordinary life." Our dear Sister had appreciated the value of this teaching; human respect never influenced her; she obeyed the inspiration of grace and thought of nothing else. While she held the office of Assistant, she one day did the penance in the Refectory of asking each of the Sisters to name her imperfections. One of our Sisters told her very simply that she abused the liberty granted to the Novices of telling their faults, and made others lose their time; that she ought to be more discreet, thinking a little of her neighbor and not of herself alone. The humble delinquent blushed; for some time after she tried to avail herself of the recommendation, but urged by the pressing solicitations of Jesus, who said repeatedly:—"Benigna, the more a soul humbles herself, the more she approaches to Me," she surrendered herself anew to the requirements of love. As she feared to fail in cordiality toward the Sister who had so charitably admonished her, Our Lord encouraged her saying that the time employed in performing an act of humiliation is not time lost, that He counts it not only for the soul herself, but also for those who practice the virtue of patience.

While we lived thus in fraternal union with our beloved Sister, her incomparable Master loaded her with marks of His divine tenderness, and continued His instructions.—"My Jesus," she asked Him one day in an outburst of gratitude, "one would say that Thou canst not live without me. What is it that attracts Thee to my soul? Then hast Thou not the Angels? Dost Thou not find Thy happiness in Thyself?"—"My Benigna," He answered, "it is true, all this is true; but it is also true that I have a human Heart, and that I love Men............I have told thee this already, but I tell thee again that thou mayst write it, my little Secretary of Love; then I will cause it to be read, that souls may believe in My excessive love; men are my brothers."

When our Most Honored Mother was fully informed of the signal favors Our Lord showered upon the dear Sister, Her Charity gave her a half-hour every day to write the divine instructions. Jesus was evidently satisfied, for we read in her notes of that time: "My Benigna, one of the means of passing unnoticed is the common life. One half-hour a day is sufficient for writing, since thou shouldst aid the Community by thy labor. I enjoy seeing thee at work in thy office, because thou art poor."

We may be permitted to cite here a charming incident which displays on one side the trusting simplicity of the young religious, and on the other the ineffable divine condescension. Here are her own words: "One day while I was aid in the linen wardrobe, I said to my Beloved: Listen, my Jesus, if you wish that I should write, it is your affair, you must arrange it. We have a great washing to extend: then tell the sun to shine so that it may dry our linen; if not, we shall have to work several days, and it is you who will lose.—Jesus in His goodness heard my prayer; the weather was perfect. However, I was not wholly satisfied; and I remarked to one of our Sisters that the favor Jesus had just granted would be still more manifest if it should rain the next day. As soon as we had taken in the washing all dried, a pouring rain came down. I was greatly embarrassed, but radiant with joy at proving once more that by confidence, we can obtain everything we wish from Our Lord." In a moment she added humbly: "The enemy tried to tempt me to pride by making me out a saint: I complained to Jesus, who told me to answer him,—With the aid of my God I will be one, because of a sinner He can make a great saint."

We have already said that our dear Sister gave her energies to the work of the linen wardrobe, but that this vast field of activity seemed little in harmony with her attractions to sweet contemplation and repose in God. No failing, however, was condoned: and as soon as she accused herself of the least inexactitude, she was severely reproved by our Most Honored Mother. One day Her Charity after having reproached her for her want of exertion, added: "Ah, my Sister, you would do well to speak of this to Our Lord; for if our Sisters did no more work than you, the Community could not get along." Our dear Sister, docile as a child, related all this to her Beloved, begging Him to make her more industrious, that she might please her good Mother:—

"Listen, my Benigna," answered Jesus, "the Community has two purses, a material purse and a spiritual purse. If I would have thee labor for the profit of the spiritual purse, the Community shall lose nothing. As long as thou art in the wardrobe I will take care that the linen wears out less; this in itself will be a profit to the material purse. Be tranquil; thy Mother shall be satisfied."

In fact, our Most Honored Mother declared that, a short time after, Sister Benigna said to her: "My Mother, if Your Charity thinks proper, we can do without the aids you have given us for our office." The surprise of our Mother can be imagined, for ordinarily the Sisters of the linen wardrobe, overtaxed with labor, never had enough assistance.

The simplicity with which our dear Sister conversed with her God enchants us so that we cannot forbear returning to her record. We read in the month of May, 1915:—"Jesus gives me all kinds of pleasures; the more my confidence in Him increases the more I enjoy the happy experience of His immense goodness. He foresees when I ought to cease or continue to write: Write one more line. He tells me, or else, Thou mayst depart; and instantly the clock strikes. To Him I abandon everything; I trust in Him for everything; I rely on Him even to awaken me in the morning; when He sees that His little Benigna is asleep, He lets her enjoy her repose till the proper moment. O how good it is to place one's self in the hands of God as a little child! What peace the soul then enjoys! The Lord has really transformed me; and this happy change is the fruit of love. For two months I have enjoyed a life of peace, of interior repose and tranquillity: this supernatural atmosphere is delicious."

The divine communications became so intimate and so habitual, that our Most Honored Mother thought it well to leave her free during the hours of silence, that she might more easily fulfill her charge of "Secretary of Jesus."

. The Divine Spouse watched ever jealously over His Beloved, that nothing of what passed in her soul might appear in the exterior. He succeeded so well that while all admired her extraordinary virtue, and experienced in her presence something indescribable that was not common to the other Sisters, it remained there; we could not penetrate farther.

We were not alone in feeling this supernatural influence; persons of the world were so affected. On one occasion among others when Sister Benigna Consolata assisted at the parlor, the mother of one of our Sisters who was there, was struck with her humble and recollected air. On returning home, she spoke of her continually with admiration and respect. Another person came one day to ask for some object belonging to the Sister whom she had seen the evening before in the parlor: "She is a saint," said she, "this object will be for me a relic." Our beloved Sister alone regarded herself ever with contempt; she likened herself to a miserable worm of the earth, who, hearing the carriage of the King pass by, cries out: "Your Majesty! Your Majesty!" then abysses herself in her nothingness, while the Sovereign Majesty deigns to stop and speak with her.

One day, annihilated at the thought of her misery, she asked her Divine Master why He lavished on her so many favors. She received this response:—"Do not seek elsewhere than in thy constant fidelity to the recommendations of obedience, the reason for the extraordinary graces I bestow upon thee. O if souls knew the value of an act of obedience!"

We can truly say that Sister Benigna Consolata carried this virtue to its highest perfection; it was, so to say, rooted in her soul, according to the testimony of the two Superiors who governed our Community during her short religious life. They could place her above or below, send her to the right or to the left, humiliate her in season and out of season, give her charges or set her aside, they were certain of finding her always humble and submissive.

"I wish thee to be faithfully faithful, my Benigna," Jesus had told her; "a little act of fidelity may be the principle of great graces. Exact observance is, as it were, a perpetual Communion for the faithful soul; for with each point of the Rule well observed, she receives an increase of grace; and when the soul receives an increase of grace, I communicate Myself to her." Our dear Sister was truly a worthy daughter of our Holy Founder; she had fully comprehended this lesson:—"Little things are little things, but fidelity in little things is a great thing." We must confess, however, that Sister Benigna Consolata was exaggerated in her exactitude, which brought upon her smart corrections. Far from becoming discouraged, she would recognize her mistake and endeavor to contain her fidelity within proper bounds. This continual application was a constant sacrifice, and the Crucified Spouse, who is pleased with suffering, assured her of His satisfaction:—"My Benigna, I love obedience so much that when I find it in a soul as it is in thine, I take My delights there. Do not let one of thy Mother's words fall to the ground. Thou dost believe Me present under the smallest fragment of the Consecrated Host; so also thou must believe that I have committed My authority to the hands of the Superior; though she were poor in natural and spiritual gifts, she holds My place as soon as she has been elected Superior; and in this case Religious have only to revive their faith as they would before a particle of the Consecrated Host."

However, after all that has preceded, it must not be thought that the favored soul of our beloved Sister was always at a feast, and that, drawn by love's force into the way of sacrifice, she did not feel the thorns. Sister Benigna Consolata had her days of indescribable suffering: she experienced disgust, dejection, weariness, as we have already shown.

We will cite a new proof from her notes of 1915:—"My Mother, Jesus is silent; He has the goodness to assure me He does it for my good—to purify me. When Jesus is silent I am like a stone, and worse still, for a stone has no distractions, while I am filled with them, as well as with defects of all kinds. Ah, then I lay my finger on my misery and see everywhere its beautiful productions. Sometimes the thought comes that I am abandoned by God; but I do not dwell on it; confidence dominates everything." Later we read; "I am always in the same disposition; I seem to be blind and deaf. No, it is not Jesus who is hidden; it is I who am blind and see Him not; I, who am deaf and hear Him not. The first days I had a desire to weep; but now I have courage and say to Jesus; *Sitivit anima mea;* or else, *Quemadmodum cervus.* My Jesus, my most sweet Jesus, I believe in Thy love; though Thou shouldst slay me, I would believe in it still. Yes, my Jesus, if I saw myself hanging by a thread above hell, and this thread were held by Thy divine hand, I would in no wise fear; even though it should break, I would not be afraid, because Thou couldst tie it together again. I know it is a great mercy on Thy part to treat me thus, for shouldst Thou deal with me as I deserve, Thou wouldst let me yield to the terrible temptations of the enemy and then strike me dead. This is what I deserve."

Yes, the infernal enemy was furious against her; as formerly he had attacked the virgin of Siena, so he assaulted this little victim of Jesus, often even during the night. When at last vanquished he abandoned the field, it was pitiful to see our poor little Sister.—Although she lost nothing of her ordinary sweetness, her pale face and exhausted frame, her sad and languid air, inspired us all with compassion; we said to one another: "What has happened to our Sister Benigna Consolata that her Charity appears to be suffering so much?" Our Most Honored Mother alone knew the wiles and struggles of the demon, who coveted this prey, so rich and beautiful. He was forever laying new snares to make her fall, and so defeat the designs of God, who destined her to unfold to the world the excess of His Mercy.

"Great changes are being operated in my soul," she writes; "I pass from a celestial peace to a sorrow the more bitter because I cannot explain it. My soul is in agony, and at the same time, by God's permission, is plunged in aridity and violently assailed by the the enemy."

We find these pages delicious—these familiar confidences of our dear Sister with her Mother.—Let us listen again: "My Mother. Jesus makes me walk in a desert. What a life I go through! True, He always says a few words to me; but they are crumbs compared with a feast. I endeavor to be recollected in order to hear Him: I am, as it were, in a solitude." And some days after: "Now Jesus speaks to me; but my soul has no more sweetness or interior unction. I am like a person who has lost the sense of taste; she eats savory dishes which nourish her, but she relishes nothing. I should like to leave this painful state; but I can do nothing but suffer without relief, consumed by a little fire. I have already experienced this pain and even more severely; it preceded, I think, the most precious graces of Jesus."

In fact, Our Lord was preparing to dictate to her sublime pages that should make known to men His ineffable tenderness; and in order to render her worthy of fulfilling her mission, He purified her in the crucible of sorrow. She would have macerated her body without mercy; her fervor would have led her to wear cilices, to fast continually, to inflict cruel disciplines; but our holy Rules moderating this kind of austerities, she indemnified herself by mortification in everything, even in the smallest things."

"My Benigna," said Jesus, "if souls had more faith, they would live on mortification as they live on bread, whereas they fly it as they would the plague." Our fervent Sister took to heart this reproach and sought every occasion of suffering. As she made progress in this way of renunciation, Jesus encouraged her to redouble her ardor:—"My Benigna, the farther thou dost advance in the way of mortification, the nearer thou wilt draw to God; it is only the first step that costs. Cast a glance upon Jesus on the Cross, and thou wilt see thy program of mortification. Spiritual consolations will be thy recompense; the more thou dost mortify the flesh, the more capable wilt thou be of comprehending the things of God. Jesus will dwell in thee according to the capacity He finds there."

The love of suffering which devoured the heart of His Benjamin was infinitely pleasing to the Crucified Spouse; he exhorted her to grant self no satisfaction:— "Treat thy body as an enemy; give it only what thou canst not refuse."

Sister Benigna Consolata, on account of her delicate constitution, had need of abundant nourishment, and often after the repast, she declared she was more hungry than when she took her seat at table. This natural tendency never served as a pretext to dispense her from mortification. She would have observed all the fasts very willingly; but this was permitted only the last year of her life, through the solicitation of Our Lord. "My Jesus, is it not to disobey if one ask for a thing that has always been refused?" "No, it is I," He answered, "who require thee to ask it; if thy Superiors do not grant permission, do what they tell thee, not what I desire; if it should be permitted, I will give thee strength to accomplish the fast." Happy in obtaining consent, she fasted strictly, and her last Lent was a time of continual graces for her soul. She saw the words of her Divine Master verified:—"My Benigna, mortification is the channel through which my choicest graces pass; if the channel is small, few graces pass; but if it is great, many graces will pass."

"Austere austerity," Our Lord said again," consists in putting a curb on nature by the bonds of rigorous mortification, enchaining it like a criminal; contradicting it in everything; if thou wouldst eat, drink; if thou wouldst drink, eat; if thou wouldst speak, be silent;

if thou wouldst be silent, speak. When in doubt as to a choice between two things, not knowing which to choose, see on which side there is more mortification; for where there is more mortification there is more perfection."

In response to the instructions of Jesus, and with the end of winning souls to Him, Sister Benigna Consolata suffered often and willingly a burning thirst. During her repasts she sometimes deprived her appetite even of necessary food, so that after Matins she would be compelled to go trembling to our Most Honored Mother and say: "My Mother, I am hungry." Our Mother, moved with pity, would get her a piece of bread; sometimes she would accept it with gratitude; but more frequently she would thank her, saying: "No, my Mother, it is enough that I have made an act of simplicity." While in bed, she always kept the same posture; and if sometimes she sought a better one, Jesus would sweetly say: "Benigna, thy Spouse on the Cross did not turn to seek a little relief!" She had ever new inventions for self-constraint and self-torment, in order to please her Well-Beloved, who rewarded the generousity of His little victim by augmenting her thirst for sufferings. At times, however, touched by the ardor of her spirit and the fragility of her body, He would say: "This is enough, Benigna; now take repose." Little by little, she obtained from her Superiors permission to converse with her good Master during two hours of the night. These colloquies, which our dear Sister has left us in writing, are delicious; and we long to hasten by our prayers the moment when these pages shall be published.

"O how I desire to love Him and be faithful to Him!" she cries out: "this desire consumes me. The more He seems to hide Himself, the more I feel I love Him; I wish so much to love Him! It is Jesus Himself who gives me this ardor, for all good comes from Him. He is silent, but His grace is destroying all the productions of my nature; I feel detached from everything, and urged to humble myself more and more. He gives me such a love of contempt that I can no longer resist the solicitations of grace."

Pursuing the course of her notes, we read:—"A state of more intimate union with God has succeeded to the interior word. I was like a child with whom its mother talks as she holds it in her arms; while now, I feel pressed to the Heart of Jesus; and in this sweet embrace Love says much. I see that the soul, and especially my soul, is nourished with God. I feel powerfully attracted, but in darting toward Him, I cry out, O my God, who art Thou and who am I? This sole thought that an infinite God permits us to love Him, ravishes me."

The blessed time during which she conversed with her incompa rable Master seemed very short to our dear Sister. Nevertheless, always faithful she was on the alert not to overstep the hour marked by obedience. We have several clocks in the Monastery; as soon as she heard the first, Sister Benigna would say simply to Our Lord that the clock had struck and their colloquy must end. Jesus would remark that it was not the Church clock and that He had yet time to say: "Nigna of gold, goodnight, adieu!" After these divine colloquies, she was so inflamed with the love of her Spouse that sometimes she could not sleep for the rest of the night; and this troubled her lest she had failed in obedience.

She was always in a state of immolation, refusing to her senses the most innocent gratifications. If our dear Sister took wings at the least sign of obedience to fulfill it, yet when there was question of learning some news, of seeing something beautiful, she was never eager, and even renounced the gratification, when she could make this little sacrifice without attracting notice. She knew how to mingle the little grain of myrrh with everything.

"Dost thou think it preferable to take thy ease rather than sacrifice it for my love?" said Jesus to her one day. "Why are there so few contemplatives, so few souls, even among religious, to whom I can impart extraordinary graces? It is because there is not enough mortification. I have sought in vain, I find very few. This does not do you honor, My spouses! I love you so much, I compassionate you; what I say to you, I say through love; for my desire is to bestow on you great graces, but I cannot do so unless you are mortified."

These sweet and powerful lessons touched the heart of our fervent Sister, who daily exerted all her strength to put them in practice. Ordinarily, she kept her eyes downcast, as we have said; even during recreation she rarely raised them. In the Choir during the holy Office, she was remarkable for her humble demeanor, devout and seriously loving, as is marked. When seated she did not lean in any way; and her feet she kept raised from the ground, which caused her real pain on account of her tall stature. During prayer she was totally absorbed in God; and in spite of weariness or of the heat, she kept her hands joined, a little removed from the breast.

Once when, overcome with fatigue, she sat down during this holy exercise, Our Lord said to her:—"Did those who accompanied me to Calvary carry seats with them?" She never did it again.

We have the pious custom in our Monastery, of making the Holy Hour every Thursday evening after Matins. Sister Benigna Consolata was always one of the most fervent. We were struck by her immobility and recollection. Compelled to fight against sleep, it happened one night that she yielded; "My Jesus, I am sleepy," she said. He answered her with ineffable tenderness, "I compassionate thee." Another time her good Master declared that if a Sister passed all the time of the Holy Hour in struggling against sleep it would be an agreeable offering, because it is sacrifice which pleases Him.

Sacrifice! It is a word repeated incessantly by the blessed lips of Jesus.

The instructions He gives our beloved Sister on this subject are found, we may say, on every page of her numerous writings.

"Benigna, few souls walk with a rapid step in the way of love, because there are very few who enter generously into the way of sacrifice. If one is constant in sacrifice, she is constant in love: if she falters in sacrifice, she falters in love. My Benigna, when there is question of sacrifice, never say, it is enough; this would mean I do not desire that love should increase in my soul. Nothing augments love in the soul like the Cross. All I ask of thee is mortification, and above all mortification of the spirit; because if exterior mortification is one of the conditions I require for the bestowal of my graces, that of the spirit is necessary to make great progress in perfection. My Benigna, with mortification thou wilt give me empty vases, which I will fill with oil; the more thou wilt give me, the more I will fill them; and when thou hast none the oil will cease."

Interior mortification was the great battle-field of our dear Sister; there she practiced self-annihilation, abandoning herself to all the requirements of divine love.

V

HER UNION WITH THE SUPER-

IOR: SUPERNATURAL GIFTS:

WAY OF CONFIDENCE AND

LOVE

Our Honored Mother guided her beloved daughter according to the desires of our Lord. On her side, Sister Benigna Consolata confided to her everything, manifesting to Her Charity the deepest gratitude. She says herself on this subject: "How I bless my Divine Master for giving me so great an opening of heart toward our Mother! After our conferences I am all inflamed with divine love. True, the enemy tries to take away my peace; but as he reveals his presence by the trouble he causes me, I do not let him disturb me."

He was furious, in fact; he dreads the perfect union of religious souls with their Superior, and hence his malice was redoubled in afflicting this generous soul. "I experienced a great repugnance once," she wrote, "in submitting to an arrangement of obedience which contradicted my will, and I almost failed in patience toward our Mother: but I went afterward and asked her pardon......My Jesus, mercy! Benigna has done as Benigna knows how to do; now do as Jesus knows how to do. I am so blind to my own faults that I do not even see them." Her Divine Spouse encouraged her in this filial union with her Superior: "My Benigna, it is through the Mother that my graces pass; if a soul is united with her Mother she receives them. Visitandines are called in a special manner to imitate my hidden life in Nazareth; and my obedience to my holy Mother is the model of the union which should exist between religious and their Superior. Yes, my Benigna, all religious ought to practice this obedience, but especially Visitandines. Be for thy Mother an open book where she can read at her pleasure." Docile to the divine lesson, Sister Benigna manifested even the least fold of her soul, with the simplicity of a child; so that our Mother compared her to one of those streamlets which, clear as crystal, show us all the little pebbles that line the watery bed.

The same childlike candor overflows in her relations with her Divine Master: "Listen, my Jesus; the Cananean woman told thee that the crumbs were for the dogs; and I come to tell thee that I would be content with those which the ants leave; for these little insects have never offended thee, and have more right than I to be fed."

Later, rendering an account of prayer, she said: "I help myself as much as I can, thinking of something that will make me advance; if I cannot think, I protest to Jesus that I love Him, and abandon myself to His will, too happy to be all His and forever, which I hope from His infinite mercy. I am always blind and deaf; but I repeat to Jesus my chant of perfect adhesion to His will, and this consoles me infinitely." A little farther: "My soul has become sad again. May the will of God be done! I trust in Thee, O Jesus! I wish so much, so much, so much to love Thee!"

If humility kept her ordinarily in profound recollection, our beloved Sister practiced no less the sweet virtue of charity. She had lost the tendency to self-will that was prominent in her childhood: and under the powerful action of grace, her character had become sweet and mild. She truly imitated our holy Founder by her amiability. "Benigna," said Jesus, "charity is sweet, but the gentleness of charity is sweeter still. Let thy words be a perfume of sweetness. I would have thee in the Monastery what the perfume is to the flower; it betrays it even in the shade. I will keep thee hidden so as to hold thee in security; but thou, My Benigna, do not forget that thy mission is to attract hearts to Me by thy sweetness."

Nothwithstanding her frequent and painful aridities, Sister Benigna Consolata was always willing to lend her services to anyone; she compassionated our little sufferings and always had the right word of consolation. In her relations with us, she carefully kept the thorns of little daily self-denials, to leave to her neighbor only the roses. We all retain a sweet memory of her exquisite charity; and if space permitted, we would relate many examples. Suffice it to say that she faithfully conformed to the program her Well-Beloved had traced out for her. "Benigna, charity must cost something; the soul must impose constant sacrifices upon herself if she would exercise charity well."

But if our dear Sister's delicacy of heart went so far as to divine our trials, our little inconveniences, our least desires, how can we estimate her tenderness and compassion for Jesus afflicted and outraged? He deigned to reveal to her the anguish of His Sacred Heart. Silent, burning tears betrayed the secret, profound sorrow of His little spouse. Often on leaving prayer or after Matins she felt an irresistible need of consolation, and with her head resting on the maternal heart, she shed a flood of tears.

We quote from the too brief Memoir of Father Piccinelli: "During the frightful war of 1914-1918, the *Confidant* of the divine secrets was urged several times by her Superiors to obtain the cessation of the terrible scourge. Jesus responded to her ardent and repeated supplications by words full of consolation. It was not a chastisement of His Justice upon the world, otherwise its sins would already have caused its destruction; it was a chastisement sent by His Mercy to save a multitude of souls running to their eternal ruin. 'One moment suffices for the Father to gain a soul,' added the Saviour........... As to those who would remain obstinate, it was mercy also to shorten their lives here below that their torments might be less dreadful in eternity. And the Divine Heart stimulated ever more and more the generous ardor of Sister Benigna Consolata for the salvation of souls, promising her that great graces would be the reward of even the smallest acts of fidelity offered for this end. At last on July 4, 1915, Jesus required of her the sacrifice of her life, *to obtain Peace according to the intentions of the Sovereign Pontiff.*"

On the morning of Shrove-Tuesday, March 7, 1916, Sister Benigna Consolata had a vision. The Sacred Heart appeared under the the form of a Heart of flesh, torn by furious dogs that outraged It horribly. She understood by this, the sorrows of Jesus during these days of disorder. Without absenting herself from the little extraordinary recreations prescribed by the Rule, she found moments to pray and console her Adorable Master, and obtained permission to make supplementary practices on that day in a spirit of expiation. In the evening Our Lord, with touching goodness, told His Benigna that He had accepted her reparation and had seen her with pleasure obey her Rule by taking part in the recreations for the love of Him.

Our dear Sister related to our Mother that while she was yet a child Jesus had told her with infinite sadness that men preferred the most contemptible things to Him, so little did they know His love; she was deeply moved and pained by it; and having then to go out through the noisy streets, she returned home without having seen or heard anything.

We have observed that her first notes were dated November, 1902. In fact, she avowed to our Mother that though in obedience she had commenced to write at that time, Our Lord had spoken to her long before. In the year 1900 she had made a temporary vow of chastity, then aged fifteen,—a vow she afterward rendered perpetual in the hands of her Confessor.

It is impossible to enumerate the treasures of graces with which our beloved Sister was favored. We would like to come to the end of her life, but we find it impossible to hasten, such precious instructions are hidden in the writings we have in our hands. On June 13, 1915, the Feast of the Sacred Heart, we read: "He said to me in a sweet, sad tone: My Benigna, give me souls! The plaintive words of my Adorable Master moved me profoundly.—How shall I give Thee souls, my Jesus?—By sacrifices, He responded. Yes, my Benigna, I would have thee in a continual state of sacrifice. When thou art not in a disposition to sacrifice thyself thou shouldst feel ill at ease· Revive this fire continually in thy heart. Souls are not saved if nothing is done for them. I died on the Cross to save them............I ask of thee no great thing—only a word withheld, a look repressed, a pleasant thought banished, in a word all that restrains and mortifies nature. These little things, united to My infinite merits, acquire a great value. If thou knewest how those souls please Me who immolate themselves in silence!"

Three days afterward He explained the martyrdom of love:— "My Benigna, in what consists the martyrdom of love? It consists in surrendering oneself to love as wood to the fire, or gold in the crucible; fire consumes the wood and reduces it to ashes; fire purifies the gold and makes it resplendent. A soul surrendered to Love can no longer interrupt the operations of Love unless by her infidelity she deprives herself of its action. As fire consumes the wood entirely, so Love continues to work until the soul has arrived at the degree of perfection which God requires of it. It suffices to surrender wholly to Love, then Love will do the rest. But remark this well: when the wood is green the fire must first consume its humidity, and this takes more time: but if the wood be dry, it is immediately consumed, and the more rapidly according as the wood is more dry. So it is with souls: those who are still full of themselves find great difficulty in yielding to the action of Love; but souls dead to themselves are quickly consumed.

"Provided I find good will in a soul, I am never weary of looking upon its miseries. My love is fed by consuming miseries; the soul that brings Me the most, if the heart is contrite and humble, is the one that pleases Me most, because she gives Me an opportunity of exercising more fully My office of Saviour. But what I wish particularly to say to thee, My Benigna, is that the soul ought never to be afraid of God, because God is all-merciful; the greatest pleasure of the Sacred Heart of thy Jesus is to lead to His Father numerous sinners; they are My glory and My jewels. I love poor sinners so much! Listen, My Benigna, My Joy, write this:—The greatest pleasure souls can give Me is to believe in My love; the more they believe in it, the greater is My pleasure; and if they wish that My pleasure should be immense, let them place no limits to their faith in My love.

"My Benigna, I will tell thee yet more of the martyrdom of Love. The soul must let itself be consumed by Love............Love is ingenious enough to know how to take everything away from the soul, without appearing to take away anything.

"Let it act, and it will despoil thee. It will commence by the exterior, as the fire first consumes the bark; then it will penetrate into the interior. Benigna, give to Love all that it asks, and never say: It is enough. The more thou givest, the more it will demand, but always with great sweetness. Love will augment in thee the desire of giving. I have very few souls surrendered so wholly to Love, because it is painful. Certain souls commence well, but turn back; they are afraid of sacrifice; I compare them to those persons who will not pluck a rose for fear they will be pricked. True love does not act so; wherever it sees a sacrifice, it darts upon it as its prey; it folds and embraces it; and the more hidden the sacrifice, the more interior and known to God alone, the more willingly is it performed. Courage, then. Tell Me thou givest Me thy will forever because thou wilt have no other movement than that of Love; then remain firm, and know that when a soul commences generously, she is always well received by My Heart. Thou mayst repair lost time by a greater fidelity in the present and especially by using the treasures of My most sweet Heart."

On July 4, 1915, with the consent of her Superiors, she made the sacrifice of her life, which Jesus had demanded:—"Love wishes to precipitate its work in thee: Love will invest thee, Love will consume thee, but with so much sweetness that while suffering the martyrdom of Love, thou wilt desire to suffer still more. My Benigna, the thirst I experience of saving the greatest possible number of souls, impels Me to seek generous ones whom I can associate in My work of love. Thou wilt be the victim of My Justice and the consolation of My Love. Thou wilt be consumed by Love. Yes, My little spouse, I accept thy sacrifice with all the expansion of My love. I will immolate thee, but it will be always with the sword of Love. I will enchain thee, but with the bonds of love. I will consume thee, but in the fire of My Love."

"On August 25, 1915," she continues, "He gave me the Decalogue of Love; the day following that of Humility; on the 31st of the same month, that of Perfection; on the 11th of September, He dictated to me the Decalogue of Confidence, and mercifully revealed to me the depth of my corruption; on the 12th, He gave me the Decalogue of Mercy, and on the 28th, the Treatise of Charity; on October 30th, I received His counsels for the time of aridity and for that of spiritual consolations. On the 7th and 12th of November, He dictated to me the *Via Crucis;* on the 24th, He instructed me on Purity of Intention."

We pause here, fearing to have been already too prolix. We shall only observe that these precious treatises, prayers, thoughts, and excerpts from the writings of our dear Sister, have been published in a little brochure entitled:—*Vade Mecum proposed to the Religious Soul by a Pious Author* (a name suggested by Jesus Himself to the Religious) a brochure that has met with general satisfaction and has already attained a wide circulation.

Referring one day to the graces which He had lavished upon her, Jesus told her that in time her writings would be printed and thus the divine favors published. "Benigna, what shall we call them?" He asked. "If the favors of Jeanne Benigne Gojos are named: *The Charm of Divine Love*, thine should bear this title:—*The Delicacies and Tendernesses of the Love of Jesus for a Little Soul.*" Another day He ended one of His divine colloquies thus:—"See how thy name is written in My most sweet Heart: *Benigna Consolata, Benjamin of the Heart of Jesus. ...*And now write the explanation of thy name under the dictate of Love:—[1]

1.—We have considered that the initial words, as they fell from the blessed lips of Jesus, would gratify the pious desires of our readers.

B.—*Bonta infinita*............Bounty of God, infinite in thy regard.

E.—*Elevati in Dio*............Elevate thy heart to God by continual acts of love.

N.—*Nega niente all'amore*............Never refuse anything to the love of thy Jesus.

I.—*Intenzione pura*............Intention most pure of pleasing God in all thou doest, in all thou sayest, in all thou thinkest, in all thou desirest.

G.—*Generosita con Dio*............Generosity towards God, generosity of love, generosity of sacrifice, generosity in action, generosity in silence. Greatness of the graces which God grants thee, although under an ordinary appearance.

N.—*Niente altro ricordo*............No longer remind Me of anything of the past except the humiliations to which thou hast submitted for My love, which I have always present to delight and please Me in thee.

A.—*Ardore nell'amore*............Ardor in love. Love Me with ardor, My little Queen. Remember that thou art eternally loved by thy God, who was made Man and died for thee.

C.—*Confidenza nel tuo Gesu*............Confidence in thy Jesus, who loves thee so much, a loving confidence, a boundless confidence.

O.—*Olocausto prezioso*............Offer thyself a precious holocaust to divine love.

N.—*Non timore*............No fear, but always love.

S.—*Spirito di sacrificio*............Spirit of sacrifice, spirit of prayer, spirit of mortification.

O.—*Offriti all'amore*............Offer thyself to the love of thy Jesus not only every day, but all the day, every minute of the day.

L.—*Loda Dio per tutti*............Laus ejus in ore meo. Praise God always for all the benefits I have bestowed upon thee.

A.—*Ardore nella preghiera*............Ardor in prayer. Let thy life, O my Benigna, be one continual prayer!

T.—*Taci per dar tempo a Dio di parlare*...... Take to heart silence and give God time to speak. Be silent and never justify thyself; be silent and never praise thyself; be silent to bury thyself in the hidden life; be silent about the arrangements of obedience; be silent regarding the operations of love, which though coming from Love, are sometimes very dolorous. Imitate the silence of Jesus: *Jesus autem tacebat.* In silence is the strength of thy interior life, because I always support the faithful soul.

A.—*Abbandono finalmente*........Abandonment, finally, My Benigna, of all thy being to the Heart of Jesus, who loves thee so much. Remember that thou art all Love's, that thou art the possession of Love."

On the 3rd of December, Jesus said to her:—"How sweet is thy name of Benigna! It is to Me like honey. If they wish to find Benigna, they must seek her in My Heart." Another time He exclaimed:—"I no longer know how to name thee. I have called thee my Lily, my Dove, My Queen; I call thee now the apple of My eye, the heart of My Heart."

On the 13th of August of the same year, (1915) before dictating to her the Decalogue of Love, He had said:—"Nigna, little Secretary of My love for My creatures, thou shalt write, others shall publish thy writings. Thine it is to taste the Gift of God in silence; others shall propagate these pages for the glory of God. Thine is the happiness of reposing on the Heart of thy Jesus while He speaks to Thee; others shall distribute these treasures; thine is the part of Mary, others that of Martha.

"Write, my Benigna, Apostle of my Mercy, write this: The principal thing I desire to make known is that I am all Love; the greatest pain souls can give Me is to doubt My goodness. Not only does My Heart feel compassion, but It rejoices when there is much to repair, provided souls have no malice. If thou couldst know how powerfully I would operate in a soul, even filled with miseries, if she would let Me! Love has need of nothing, but it must find no resistance. Often all that is required of a soul to render it holy, is to let Me act. Imperfections cannot displease Me, unless the soul loves them. She should use them as so many steps of the ladder to mount to Me by means of humility, confidence and love; I descend to the soul that humbles herself, and go to seek her in her nothingness to unite Myself to her.

"The whole secret of sanctity lies in these two words; distrust and trust. Distrust always in thyself, but not stopping there, rise immediately to trust in God; for if I am good to all, I am especially good to those who trust in Me. Knowest thou what souls profit most by My goodness? Those who trust the most. Trusting souls are the robbers of My graces. Write that the pleasure I take in the trusting soul is inexpressible.

"As the fire is fed with combustibles, and increases according as they are supplied, so My mercy is nourished with the miseries it consumes, and the more it receives the more it increases. O My Benigna, if men knew how I love them and how My Heart rejoices when they believe in My love! They believe in it too little, too little!

"They know not the wrong they do to God in doubting His divine goodness! Sins may be enormous and numerous; but provided that the soul returns to Me, I am always ready to pardon all, to forget all. Thou art the Apostle of the Mercy of God; I have made choice of thee that thou mayst become the channel of the Divine Mercies.

"Write then that I make the most beautiful masterpieces with the most miserable subjects, provided they will let Me. When a soul repents of her faults and deplores them, thinkest thou I am so hard as not to receive her? If so, thou knowest not My Heart. My most loving Heart has such a thirst for the salvation of souls, that when they return to Me I cannot contain my joy; I run to meet them. The greatest injury the demon can cause a soul after having made it fall into sin, is to incite it to distrust. As long as a soul has confidence, her return is easy; but if the demon succeeds in closing the heart with distrust, O how I have to struggle to reconquer it!

"Write, my Benigna, that all may know this: It is certain that a hundred sins offend Me more than one alone; but if this single sin is distrust of Me, it wounds My Heart more than the hundred others, because distrust wounds My Heart to its innermost core. I love men so much!

"Yes, they have too narrow an idea of the goodness of God, of His mercy, His love for His creatures. They measure God by creatures, and God has no limits; His goodness is without bounds. O that men are able to use God and will not do it! Why is this? Because the world knows Him not. I am an infinite treasure which My Father has placed at the disposal of all. They who reject Me will comprehend their misfortune only in Eternity. I love men; I love them tenderly as My dear brethren; although there is an infinite distance between them and Me, I make no account of it.

"Thou canst not conceive the pleasure I take in fulfilling My Mission of Saviour. When sins have been pardoned, they become for the soul fountains of graces because they are perpetual sources of humility. Everything contributes to the advancement of a soul, everything; even her imperfections are in My divine hands like so many precious stones, because I change them into acts of humility, which I inspire the soul to make. If those who build houses could transform the debris and all that obstructs their work into materials of construction, how fortunate they would consider themselves! Well, the faithful soul does this with the aid of My divine grace; and her faults, even the gravest and most shameful, become fundamental stones of the edifice of her perfection."

We are truly at the source of living waters, at the blessed fountains of the Saviour. May these refreshing and marvellous waters soon have their free course! They will bear, we sweetly trust, abundant fruits of grace and salvation.

But let us return to our dear Sister:—"I was plunged in the consideration of my nothingness, seeing in myself so many miseries," she writes, "when I heard Jesus say sweetly to me:—Sell them to My Mercy! Another day, I had placed a statuette of the Infant Jesus near the sheet of paper on which I was writing; a light movement I made caused it to fall. I raised it immediately and gave a kiss to the little Jesus, saying to Him; If you had not fallen you would not have had that kiss.[1] And He answered me with incredible sweetness:—It is just the same, My Benigna, when thou hast committed an ivoluntary fault; thou dost not offend Me; but the act of humility and love thou makest deliberately afterward, is the kiss thou givest Me, which I would not have received hadst thou not committed that imperfection."

We cannot but be astounded at the tenderness and familiarity of a God toward His little creature! We may say that there is not a single place in our Monastery that has not been a witness of these divine

---

1.—"Adest dilectus, amovetur magister, rex disparet, dignitas exuitur, reverentia ponitur. Cedit quippe fastus, ubi invalescit effectus. Et sicut quondam quasi amicus ad amicum Moyses loquebatur, et Dominus respondebat: ita et nunc inter Verbum et Animam, ac si inter duos vicinos familiaris admodum celebratur confabulatio. (St. Bernard, Serm. XLV in Cant.)

"Once the Beloved is present the Master disappears, the King vanishes, Majesty is effaced, awe laid aside. Transcendence in truth yields where love grows strong. And as of old, like friend to friend, Moses spake and the Lord answered, so even now between the Word and the Soul, as if between two familiar neighbors, the most intimate converse prevails."

71

confidences. The cell in which our dear Sister received the instructions and caresses of the Divine Master is a sacred place for us. Did not He Himself tell His beloved to consider it a Sanctuary?

If it is sweet to refresh our souls with these precious teachings of Jesus, it is not without emotion that we read the numerous renditions of prayer of His humble chosen one. The ardent love she bore her Well-beloved is revealed in its fullness, while her soul is unveiled with a simplicity that is enchanting, in that she touches with a certain sublime artlessness the summits of the highest perfection. We come to the opening of the year 1915:—"Today Jesus demanded; My Benigna, wouldst thou have Me tell thee of thy interior state?— I do not know, my Jesus; do as Thou wilt.—Very well, write: My interior state is a state of peace, of confidence and love; my repose is God, my desire is God."

She adds:—"The prayer that Jesus has taught me is very sweet; the soul is not fatigued; it is nourished and at rest as if she saw." And another time:-"Jesus becomes ever more sweet in His guidance of me..........He fills me with Himself..........I have a continual thirst for prayer; I have a thirst for spiritual reading, but above all, I have a thirst for Jesus. There are moments in which I feel an immense need of God, an ardent desire to love Him for all those who love Him not, to supply for what they will not do for Him. I do not see God, but I feel Him, and I would like to die to be united to Him."

At the end of this year (1915), during the days which preceded the Feast of Christmas, as we were talking in recreation of the approaching Solemnity, Our Lord murmured in her ear: "This will be thy last Christmas; I am going to take thee to Paradise."

In January, 1916, the last year of her life, our dear Sister disclosed her heart on this subject:—"During these days I feel an excessive desire of Heaven. I am like a person impatient to depart on a beautiful journey. Yes, my beloved Mother, if Jesus no longer lets me hear His voice, perhaps it is because He is going to call me to Himself so soon. I know not, but I love Him so much, that during the night when I awaken, my thought and my heart fly to my God. O happy moments, in which the soul sighs after God, hears God, is fed with God! A hunger for prayer devours me, and my occupations not permitting me to practice it during the day with the ardor which Jesus gives me, I feel the need of supplying for it during the night. If anyone were to ask me:—Benigna, what dost thou desire? I would answer: Heaven! I desire to go to my God. I desire to be always in prayer; I desire to be one with God; this is why it is painful to speak with creatures, because I am in a celestial atmosphere, and feel the need still more of sacrificing myself in the future."

In the month of February, Sister Benigna Consolata relapsed into aridity. "Jesus is silent, and my helplessness increases," she writes. "My soul tries in vain to excite a little fervor; I see in myself only miseries and infidelities............My Jesus, mercy!"

The short visits of the Saviour brought to her ineffable happiness; then anew came darkness and desolation to invade her soul. "I am like a tree stripped of its fruits. Jesus, *fiat* always! All for love. My Jesus, give me Thyself, then take away all the rest. May Thy Holy Name be blessed!" Some time after she records: "In this painful state I do not lose the presence of God; I pray, I make aspirations, but the good Jesus is silent. However, He Himself makes me love this suffering, for it glorifies Him; yes, pure love ought to make it preferable to divine consolations. My Jesus, render me strong, generous and constant in Thy love. As a proof of Thy divine presence, Thou sheddest in my soul a delicious peace; the enemy tries hard to trouble it; but, O Jesus! if Thou dost guard Benigna, she is in safety."

After these long and painful days of trial, borne with admirable resignation, after the frightful assaults of Satan, furious at seeing this sweet victim snatch from him so great a number of souls, Jesus comes to console her: "My Benigna, the measure is full, thou hast put on the last grain."—"My Jesus, what is it that leads Thee to speak to me again?"—"Benigna, it is the humiliation of thy soul and thy constant fidelity in spite of aridity; if Thou findest no joy in it, I find it, Benigna."—"My Jesus, how couldst Thou suffer this state to last so long a time?"—"It was for thy good; I wish to prepare thee to receive new graces; I have taken away consolations so as to give thee an opportunity to pratice perfect charity. One *Ave Maria* said without sensible fervor, but with a pure will in time of aridity, has much more value in My eyes, than an entire Rosary recited in the midst of consolations. Write this for the comfort of souls."

Some days after, she adds:—"Jesus tells me that after His grace, the Cross is the most precious gift He can make to a soul."

In these precious notes we are struck especially by the complaints of God, the pressing appeals of His loving Heart, which becomes a mendicant for the love of His creatures.—"O my Benigna! be the Apostle of my love! Cry aloud so that all the world may hear, that I hunger, I thirst, I die to be received by My creatures. I am in the Sacrament of My love for My creatures, and they make so little ac count of it! O do thou at least, My Benigna, make as many spirit ual communions as possible to supply for the Sacramental Commun ions which are not made. One every quarter of an hour is not enough. Make them shorter, but more numerous. If a wife saw her spouse dying of hunger, she would go from door to door to beg for Him. My Benigna, seek to draw souls to receive Me in Holy Communion. What I say to thee, communicate to thy Mother. Thou art the Apostle of My love; but when thy body shall be under the earth, and thy soul in Heaven like a little atom in My Heart for all eternity, then it will be thy Mother who will make known to souls what thou shalt have written."

Again He says:—"O My Benigna! what gives Me most pain is to see the indifference, the hatred they have for Me. They fly from Me as they would fly from a robber or an assassin; from Me, who ask only to replenish souls with My graces: but I cannot do it because they do not desire them......My Benigna, I thirst for the love of My creatures. The Seraphim love Me ardently, the saints love Me, and their love is pure and perfect. I have great love in Heaven, yet I come to earth to seek it because on earth their love is free." As Jesus saw His Benjamin afflicted at what she had just heard, He consoled her:—"Benigna, I have good souls, even in the world; and in them I take My delight. They are the oases in which I repose in the midst of the desert."

VI

RETREAT OF LOVE: HER SOL-

EMN PROFESSION WITH LOVE

The Happy confidant of the Heart of Jesus and the incessant laments of His love, unknown and outraged, could no longer live here below; she sighed ardently after the eternal union. The divine Lover, who was preparing to consume His dear victim, wishing to purify her more, invited her to make a retreat, during which He Himself would be her Director.

"Ask permission of thy Mother," said He, "to withdraw into solitude from the eve of the 20th of June to July 2 inclusively." Our dear Sister remarked that this would make twelve days, whereas our annual retreats last only ten; but Our Lord answered, "Twelve days are not too much to prepare thee for death." On June 19th, at the Obedience, our Honored Mother announced that Sister Benigna Consolata would enter into retreat. Everyone embraced her affectionately, recommending herself to her fervent prayers. We all wished her a good retreat and a speedy return. Alas! she was to return to us for so short a time! Sweet and smiling as usual, she gave us marks of affection, assuring us of her prayers, while her face was radiant with happiness.

Love attracted her. Like a dove she was to retire into the hollow of the rock with her Well-Beloved, to learn to know Him better and to love Him more. From the first, Sister Benigna Consolata descended into the abyss of her misery, not to indulge in a disquieting repentance, but to be established in the plenitude of peace, in the certainty of divine pardon and of the predilection of Jesus for her soul.

Her heavenly Director left her some days in the purgative life, trying her sweetly and gently. Before all He wished to break off her habit of self-inspection, of exaggerating her troubles, of re-

75

peating her examens, made up of a thousand little nothings, etc.—
"In the Meditation of the Creation this morning," she writes, "I saw
what a mistake a servant would make who would prefer to be sweep-
ing or dusting, when her Master wished she should be taking care
of the children............I am the servant of the Lord; I ought, therefore, to prefer my Master's will to my own. Now, His will is that
I should devote my attention to souls, and set aside my own interests
to take care of His. When I had finished this Meditation, He
deigned to favor me with a conference.—My Benigna, He said,
there is an apostolate of the interior life, of immolation, of the hidden life: it is that of the Visitation............I am raising an army and
I call souls to combat for Love. The most generous are those who
serve in the first line............My Benigna, I am going to explain this
great word, annihilation. Annihilation means death. A thought
comes which pleases thee; banish it, forget it, and it is the death of
that thought; sacrifice a desire, and it is the death of that desire;
when thou hast a will to do something and renouncest it, it is the
death of that will; every act of death is an act of life, because the
moment thou diest to nature thou livest to God.

"The third Meditation today is still on the same subject—the
Creation. I have seen how God created me in preference to so many
souls who would have loved Him better than I have done, and this
view touched me deeply. I represented to myself a great Lord who,
free to take into his service a very capable domestic, would choose
in preference a poor blockhead who would let his meat burn, break
his dishes, etc., and keep her through charity in spite of all her waste
and destruction. Is not this my portrait? Ah! how many graces I
have lost and let fall to the ground! How many lights Jesus has
given me, especially on the interior life, of which I have not profited
because of my negligence!"

June 21.—"Today Jesus said to me:—Keep thy eye fixed on God.
The more closely a soul is called to follow Me, the more mortified
she should be. Perfect despoilment is the most necessary condition
for union with God. To despoil oneself of an object is to leave it
and never to take it again. So one must forsake her imperfect hab-
its as she would cast aside a worn out garment never to wear it again.
Clothe thyself with new garments which Love has prepared for
thee. During this retreat I am making thee a trousseau which thou
wilt have only to receive from My hand; above all, I wish to trace
for thee a special plan of humility, intense humility. When a soul

is called here below to converse with God, she ought to be clothed with humility as God is clothed with glory.—My Jesus, what shall I do?—I am going to explain to thee, My Benigna; thou art the Benjamin of Love. Thou shouldst be clothed with humility, that is, all in thee should breathe humility. Humility will lead thee never to judge anyone; humility will lead thee to regard thyself as the servant of all; humility will lead thee ever to accuse thyself. When a soul has been introduced by Love into this profound abyss of humility, she walks securely and makes progress, for nothing can stop her."

On the same day she writes: "This morning Jesus said:—Thou hast acted with a peace which ravishes My Heart; thou hast acted like a daughter of Love. My Benigna, thou knowest a little thorn may make a great rent, but if one is careful to take it out immediately, it leaves scarcely a trace. When thou art afraid of having displeased me, say at once; My Jesus, if I have offended thee in anything, grant me the grace to repair it; and deign to enlighten me that another time I may better accomplish thy will. My Benigna, all that I do in thee is done with the end of establishing thee in peace. If God is to act in a soul He must find it in peace. When thou art not in peace thou neither hearest Me nor feelest My presence, and yet I am in thee.—My Jesus, thou canst do all things, wilt Thou not take away my troubles?—No, My Benigna, because in taking them away, I would deprive thee of many graces. When I permit temptation, it is not through cruelty, but to give the soul an opportunity of merit. My love has a thousand inventions for enriching souls. The perfume of the lily differs from that of the carnation. I who am the Prince of Peace give thee the perfume of peace. Since thou receivest Me in thy heart every day in the Holy Communion, let all in thee exhale the perfume of peace............ I wish to give thee eyes to fix them on God, to fly to Him, in order that thou mayst dwell in the heights.

"My Benigna, write:—Sanctity is composed of a multitude of little acts..........God, on His side, favors the soul with a multitude of graces to which she ought to correspond faithfully..........Do not think that to make a good retreat thou art obliged to meditate on hell. Thou wilt make this Meditation, but with Me in an atmosphere of love. The fruit thou must draw is a burning zeal to hinder souls from falling there. Moreover, in the Meditation the soul should appropriate only that which suits her. If thou make the considerations on hell rigorously, without striving to reform what is imperfect in thee, thou wilt go out of the retreat just as thou didst enter it, whereas thou shouldst be transformed. I have already told thee that this retreat is not only for thee, but for souls. It is true that thou wouldst enjoy thy solitude better if thou wert not to write; but he who makes a book does not keep the manuscript for himself; he has it printed that all the world may have it; so also, My Benigna, will thy writings be printed and will do good to a multitude of souls, which will augment thy accidental glory in Paradise.

"Wouldst thou give Me pleasure? Take the pen a moment and write: Annihilation of the creature before God is the summit of perfection. When a soul has arrived at such a point as to delight in self-contempt for the love of her God, she has attained the height of perfection. Benigna, when I find a soul who is willing to let Me do in her all that I desire, that soul becomes My Benjamin."

On the following day, our dear Sister continues thus:—"Benigna," said Jesus, "now let us commence prayer. Thy interior state ought not to alarm thee; it is known to Love, willed by Love, and ruled by the Love of a God. It seems to thee, My Benigna, that thou seest nothing, that thy soul goes from precipice to precipice; but it is not so. Has he who is borne by another any need of seeing? These moments are painful, but they are necessary; they are the moments of God, and the soul can do nothing better than to resign herself, believe, adore and love............Believe in love and thou wilt understand. A Religious is obliged to become holy, less for herself than to increase the glory of God. It is not an optional thing, but an obligation; thou shouldst attain to sanctity, thou and the other Religious. Now, in what does sanctity consist? In becoming as far as possible the living image of thy Spouse. Copy Me, copy Me constantly, and therefore have the eyes of thy soul ever fixed upon thy Jesus. To copy Me, I will that thou seek no other means than holy Observance. If thou art faithful to Observance according to the spirit, it will be easy to imitate Me in everything; but for this one must have the interior spirit.—My Jesus, do me the charity to break this bread to me, for I wish to commence seriously.

"My Benigna, it is the Directory that leads the soul to the Constitutions; the Directory will vivify all thy actions. To be living, an action must be animated with the interior spirit. Count some of the actions thou dost in one day. If thou knowest how to vivify them all by the faithful practice of the Directory, what merits are amassed in a single day! This is the hidden life, in which she who disappears the most, bears the most fruits."—"And how shall I hide myself?" "By silence and humility. Robbers generally steal in the night so as not to be seen; so also do thou seek the night of the common life to pass unperceived. Nothing hides a soul so well as the common life, not only from the eyes of others, but from her own eyes. The soul seeing nothing, believes she does nothing; but she does much more than if she accomplished extraordinary things.

"Write, My Benigna: Let thy look be that of Jesus, always sweet and serene; and when thou art suffering interior trials, be as smiling as when thou beholdest Me with an intellectual view. This costs the soul, but here is found true virtue. As to thy exterior, if thou wilt have it resemble that of Jesus, plunge thyself in the consideration of thy nothingness; or, if thou wilt, in the remembrance of thy general confession; this will give thee a touch of humility; make the trial of it, whatever be thy resolution............I am going to give thee a spiritual bouquet, whose fragrance thou canst inhale the whole day: *Whoever wishes to find me must seek me in the Heart of my Jesus. I am buried in the abyss of the Mercy of my Jesus."*

As we progress in this marvellous Retreat of Love, we read again: —"My Benigna, I am going to speak a word of Love, not a word of rigor, of justice, but a word of sweetness, of peace and consolation. Prepare for thy Solemn Profession with the Love of an infinite God, All-Powerful, All-Merciful. My Infinity will attract to itself all thy miseries and consume them in an instant; My Omnipotence will not only consume them, but will change them into so many precious stones, and My Mercy will effect great things in thy soul."

On June 28 she writes:—"Sometimes during our prayer Jesus keeps me sweetly absorbed in Him, my only Love. He is so liberal that He floods me with His divine light even in the smallest details; so that I am still with the Blessed Jesus in the Garden of Olives.— What ought I to do, O Jesus, write the beautiful things Thou hast told me, or else of this prayer?—I would have thee write also of this prayer; it is always instructive for souls and shows them what need they have of breaking the Holy Gospel to pieces, of tasting it and digesting it. They should live of the Gospel, as they live on the air, on light, on food. Write as well as thou canst and I will make thy way of prayer understood."

"Yesterday evening, Jesus had the goodness to give me these

words as a point of Meditation:—Dost thou betray the Son of Man with a Kiss?—Then I received a special light on these other words of the Blessed Jesus:—If you seek me, let these go their way.—I would have preferred the last subject, but Jesus told me amiably that the first sufficed.—By a kiss!—What is a kiss, then? A kiss is a sign of love; and yet Judas used it to betray Jesus. O how many times, under pretext of love for Jesus, have I assured myself in my examen that I had not willed to offend my Lord, and consequently there could be no sin! And in all these windings of self love which fetter the action of Divine Love in my soul, behold a kiss! There is an appearance of love and it is an act of treason. O Jesus, I thank Thee for having given me a light so salutary! I thank Thee, my Jesus! Judas, in kissing the most Adorable Saviour, did not wound Him, did not bruise Him, even slightly; yet with that kiss he made the first link in the chain of sufferings which began for Jesus in the Garden of Olives and ended by the death of the Cross! The Passion was the consequence of a kiss. O my Jesus, what a lesson! Who can measure the consequences of one little act? Thou hast shown them to me this morning. When I write I would like sometimes to add things which would turn to my advantage, but I have the light not to do it; I obey the inspiration with the intention of hindering, if possible, the diffusion of bad reading, or at least of preventing an author from inserting a pernicious article in his journal.

"Then Jesus said to me:—Every time thou hearest the clock strike, if it be not during an exercise, fall on thy knees in order to break thy will; thou canst only gain by it, for thus thou shalt be separated from the mire of earth and fly to the arms of God. O my Benigna, if souls had more faith, how much better they would understand virtue! If there are few saints it is because there are few mortified souls............They ought to live on mortification as they live on bread, whereas they fly it as they would the plague............But now I will leave thee to continue thy prayer.

"That journal, into how many hands it will fall! And thanks to an act of fidelity," continues our dear Sister, "I may be the cause of one evil article the less in its pages............How sad it is to think that by our immortification and self seeking we may be guilty, so to say, of much evil which would not be committed if we had the generosity to conquer ourselves and thus draw down the divine light and grace upon souls!"

On June 30, 1916, the Feast of the Sacred Heart of Jesus, Sister Benigna Consolata, at the solicitation of her Divine Spouse, made her Solemn Profession with Love, in the presence of His Lordship, Monsignor our Bishop, and of our Most Honored Mother. She read aloud the formula of renovation of her Holy Vows: the Vow of doing all for Love, the Vow of Abandonment, the Sacrifice of her Life, the Vow of Perfection, and the Vow of Humility. The Sacrifice of her Life was not a vow in the beginning; she had made the offering in July, 1915; but in September of that year she changed the offering into a vow.

How can we portray the admirable dispositions of our dear Sister on that beautiful day! How tell her generous and heroic correspondence to the least impulse of grace! How convey the love of God which invaded and consumed her heart! How conceive the ineffable tendernesses of divine love shed upon her soul with a plenitude measureless and indescribable! Let us leave to her the office of revealing the secrets of Love, and draw some brief points from her memorandum of June 30:—

"Jesus is always Jesus. It would take too long to write all He did for me on this blessed day; and if I speak of it, may the glory be His alone!—Benigna, He said, write for the glory of My Heart; for when an artist makes beautiful things out of the meanest materials, all the glory reverts to Him.—I have spent this happy day in the most profound peace; Jesus has set me at liberty, convincing me that my five private Vows will not be an increase of trial to me, but rather a means of deliverance; and He has explained them to me.

"I asked Him afterward what He desired of me. He answered: —Thou hast eyes then read: What is here written in My Heart? LOVE ME! If thou lovest Me, thou wilt repair; if thou repairest, thou wilt console Me; and then thou wilt be a faithful spouse: LOVE, REPARATION, CONSOLATION, FIDELITY. My Benigna, thou canst never love Me with all thy heart, as I wish to be loved by thee, unless thou dost hate thyself with all thy heart. Sacrifice thy personal interests and gratifications to the greater glory of God. Thou wilt not be truly a repairer if thou art content to gaze superficially on the wounds sinners make in My Heart; they must be examined closely. Sinners hate Me; do thou love Me with all thy strength; sinners blaspheme My Holy Name; do thou praise Me; sinners banish Me from their memory; do thou keep Me ever present before thy mind, discarding every other thought. Let all thy actions bear the impress of Reparation and thou wilt console My Heart. Let thy life be a life of Love and Reparation. I wish to live in thee in this Monastery; I wish to see with thy eyes, to speak with thy mouth, to hear with thy ears, to walk with thy steps, to labor with thy hands·

"Today, June 30, 1916, is the day of thy Espousals with the God of Love, the God of Goodness, the God of Mercy. My Benigna, until now thou hast walked in the narrow way of fear, of trials, of anguish, of affliction of heart; My love planned this way; it had chosen it for thee; but in espousing the God of Love, the God of Peace, the God of Sweetness, thou wilt participate in the glory of God."

Some days after, she records His words:—"My Benigna, spouse of Eternal Love, thou hast been introduced into the Cabinet of the Spouse; if thou wilt not cease to be the *Prediletta* of God, the Favorite of God, the Benjamin of God, thou must destroy nature by a rigorous mortification. Do not be frightened by what I am going to say to thee: When Love takes possession of a soul it is with a sort of amorous fury. A leaf carried away by the wind no longer touches the earth, it flies with the rapidity of the wind; so it is with a soul which has become the prey of Love; she goes whither Love carries her, and is never dragged below by her infidelities............Benigna, God speaks to thee, God instructs thee, God loves thee!"

A little farther we read:—"As I attested to our Lord my desire to make His Mercy known to souls, He deigned to reply: Yes, thou canst do it; thy writings are destined to make it known. Every word thou writest is a chanter of my Mercy. Write as much as possible, since I wish to make use of thee, poor little nothing."

"Today, July 7th, having gone to make a Visit to our Sacramental Jesus, He said to me suddenly :—'Go, my Benigna, because here thou enjoyest me, but there thou lovest Me.'—This is when I write; it pleases Jesus so much."

"Arrived at the summit of perfection," writes Father Piccinelli in his eulogy of his saintly daughter, inundated with divine graces and favors, Sister Benigna Consolata, a true daughter of Holy Mary, lost nothing of her self-effacement in the Community. We can indicate only two of her companions whose notice she attracted. 'Sister Benigna Consolata, where did you learn the beautiful things you tell us in the Assembly after Vespers?' one of these two nuns asked her one day. 'From a PIOUS AUTHOR,' she answered unmoved. Jesus had suggested to her this response. And there investigations ceased."

While the Divine Spouse favored His little Benjamin, the wicked spirit with satanic hatred left no means untried to wrest her from Love and make her his own. If his temptations had *always been frightful and tremendous,* now he assailed her with a fury so *vehement* that she was *crushed.* The fear of her eternal condemnation and all that it implies most cruel and terrible, took possession of her mind and heart, and not able to bear up against it, she went all trembling and exhausted to take refuge near our Mother. In vain Her Charity strove to calm her, reminding her of the divine predilection of Jesus for her soul, and the sweet names He had so often given her. "Ah, my Mother!" she exclaimed, melting into tears, "it seems to me all a dream; and if it were true, how many graces I have abused!" At last our Mother succeeded in repulsing the attacks of the enemy, and Sister Benigna Consolata, again calm and smiling, re-entered into the way of Love. On the same evening, our Lord told her that our Mother had merited more in accomplishing this act of exquisite spiritual charity, than if she had fasted a whole year on bread and water, so ardently He desires that souls should walk in the way of confidence and love, and shun the perilous rocks of distrust.

Our beloved Sister was not to remain long with us. But before she was attacked by the inexorable disease which conducted her rapidly to the tomb, our Lord willed to give her a sweet consolation, that of seeing once more her former Director, the Reverend Canon Boccardo, whom she had not seen from her entrance into the Monastery.

"Write to him to come quickly; if he delays, he will regret it," Jesus had said to His little Secretary during her Retreat; and the latter sent him the divine message. The Canon Boccardo responded at once to the pressing invitation. He came, bearing with him the notes written by our dear Sister when she was in the world, which he had piously preserved.

Great was the joy of the venerated Director and his dear daughter in meeting again. Sister Benigna Consolata would have been glad to open her whole soul to him who understood her so well and to whom she owed so much; to tell him the history, day by day, of those nine years; to review with him the way she had travelled, now sown with flowers, now bristling with the thorns of temptation, to point out the rents made in the mantle of her perfection by the briers of self-inspection and her perpetual uncertainties. But the prudent Director needed not to learn all this; he was satisfied to find her on the Mount of Lovers in the arms of Jesus. With gentle firmness he cut short all these reviews, preferring to employ those hours in heart-to-heart spiritual colloquies. It is easy to conjecture that the Angels deputed to guard our Monastery must have beheld burning flames arise, as formerly above the Convent where St. Benedict and St. Scholastica held their last heavenly colloquy. But time pressed; the Canon Boccardo arrived in Como on the evening of July 5, and remained only the day following, the First Friday of the month. Before his departure, with the permission of our Most Honored Mother, he exchanged crucifixes with Sister Benigna Consolata, happy to bear away a souvenir of his dear daughter, who was to feast on the First Friday of September, not in this land of pain and tribulation, but in the Celestial Country amid the fullness of eternal joy and love.

We were eager to welcome once more our angelic Sister, to inhale again the fragrance of her sweet virtues. O how long these twelve days of retreat seemed to us! Yet when she returned to the Community, we were all seized with an indescribable emotion. She seemed wholly under the dominion of the supernatural, something divine radiating from her personality, to such a point that several Sisters, through respect, dared not approach to embrace her, but contented themselves with expressing lovingly their happiness in seeing her again. It is written that Moses, after having conversed with God on the mountain, had to veil the glory of his countenance, the people being unable to look upon its splendor; and our dear Sister admitted to such close converse with the Spouse, appeared to us to be enveloped in a veil of modesty and self-contempt; but this veil was not thick enough to conceal entirely the marvels which the God of glory and love had operated in her. They divined that Sister Benigna Consolata had given place to an invisible and mysterious Being, who prayed, spoke, labored, recreated, in a word, acted in her and for her. We felt that her beautiful soul was being detached, little by little, from her body; material things no longer touched her, although she performed with unvarying fidelity all the details of her daily duties. She pined to see her mortal ties broken, that free at last, she might fly to her Well-Beloved. The fire of love had long since consumed her; the flame went on increasing, and the sweet victim wasted away, day by day, exciting in our hearts serious apprehensions.

We have said that our dear Sister had permission to hold sweet converse during the night with her God; but two hours would no longer suffice; now three, four, five hours flew by, swift as lightning, for the happy Benjamin of Jesus. We questioned one another if the frail envelope could long hold out, if the angelic soul was not soon to take its flight to Heaven, the object of her ardent desires. Alas! our fears were too well founded. Toward the end of the month of July, Sister Benigna Consolata was attacked with the disease which was to bear her away from us after a month of cruel sufferings.

One day, not having been able to communicate, she complained of her coldness and indifference; but her Divine Master comforted her:—"It is not indifference in thee, since during the night when thou wert so ill, thou wert preparing to do My will; and I gave thee many graces by thy spiritual Communion, although thou couldst not receive that which is proper to the Sacrament. A soul who is always united to My will through love, makes, so to say, a perpetual Communion."

"My interior disposition," she writes, "is that of a profound peace. Jesus is detaching me from everything, even from the most holy things, as Confession and Holy Communion............It is not that I esteem them less, but abandonment to God and union with His adorable will cause mine to be so lost in His that I can no longer find it."

VII

HER LAST ILLNESS; AFTER

THE DARKNESS, ETERNAL

LIGHT

On the 3rd of August, our dear Sister changed her cell for the Infirmary. On reaching the gallery called the Tribune, where the sick Sisters hear Mass, she entered with a tottering step to make a little Visit to her Jesus, offering herself anew as a victim to His love and His divine good pleasure. The three first days she was deprived of Holy Communion; but after the First Friday, It was borne to her every morning until her death. Once as she lamented her want of fervor in preparing to receive her God, He deigned to console her:—"Benigna, the best preparation thou canst make, is to trust in Me. To love Me as a spouse is more easy, to suffer as a spouse is more meritorious; thy sufferings will go on increasing. Thou must needs lend Me thy body for suffering; and I will send thee great interior trials, to give thee the merit of cutting them short by obedience."

In fact, the sufferings of our beloved patient were augmented every day. Anguish of spirit and terrible attacks of the demon were added to her physical sufferings. Her frequent fainting spells were followed by convulsions. She experienced acute pains, especially in the left shoulder, while she was always in a burning fever. She said often to our Mother:—"O my Mother, how I suffer! but I am happy." And again:—"The little lamb is on the funeral pyre, and the flames are beginning to scorch her." One evening we saw her suddenly seized with profound emotion; she melted into tears, and on our inquiring the cause, she answered:—"I weep because I see Jesus, who is doing Himself violence to make me suffer; He is forced to it, having chosen me for a victim; but it costs Him to hide from me His love." Then, looking with ineffable tenderness upon a picture of the Sacred Heart:—"I know Thou lovest me, O Jesus! I believe in Thy love for me!"

Our Lord foretold to her a *night of great sufferings*, and spoke to to her at length of the efficacy of holy water to repulse the attacks of the infernal spirit, adding that the presence of the Superior who, in virtue of her charge, is like the Ostensorium of God, would be for her a shield of defense. Another time He told her that in absence of the Superior, she should be surrounded by her Sisters, for, being the temples of the Holy Ghost, they would protect her powerfully.

On the 14th, she expressed a desire to receive Extreme Unction; she prepared for it with great fervor and received it with joy on the same day, at two o'clock in the afternoon. She begged Jesus to make her suffer still more.—"Yes, *my Jesus, still more,*" she said; "*beat, beat Thy ass, but give me souls,* and close hell so that no one may ever fall into it. O if I knew that by suffering, not only during weeks, months, years, but even to the end of the world, if possible, I could glorify my God and save souls for Him, meriting nothing, it seems to me that I would willingly endure all sorts of afflictions; not alone, but with Jesus always near me, assisting me and speaking to me continually. He often calls me, My Nigna, My Joy."

On the evening of the same day, Monsignor our Bishop visited her. She could not cease expressing to him her happiness in suffering and in suffering for love, adding that this day she was suffering for priests. This great inebriation of joy in suffering lasted till toward the 20th of August; she had prayed Jesus on the First Friday of the month to grant her grace to suffer cheerfully, and she had obtained it. Indeed, she had never appeared so bright and cheerful as during her sickness. Always sweet and cordial, yet she had been serious and concentrated. As soon as she was settled in the infirmary, she took on a gayety and amiability that charmed us·

On the Feast of the Assumption, Sister Benigna Consolata saw all the Community. She begged us to chant the canticle:

"*Al ciel, al ciel, al ciel,*	"To Heaven, to Heaven, to Heaven,
Andro a vederla un di—	I go to see Her one day,—
La dolce Madre mia,	The lovely Madre mia,
Andro veder Maria."	I go to see Maria!"

And while the Sisters with anguish in their hearts and the chant upon their lips, gratified her desire, she was radiant with happiness. Smiling sweetly, she bade adieu to all as if she were going to a Feast long sighed-for and most dear.

But before crossing the threshold of eternity, she had to traverse terrible hours, hours of darkness, of supreme purification. The conflict commenced. At first there were doubts on the predilection of Jesus for her soul, fears that she had deceived Superiors in speaking of the "Voice," fears that her writings were all lies, her life an imposture. Obedience alone had power to restore her to peace; but when calm returned she was exhausted, prostrate, like a warrior after a long combat. "My Mother," said she, "Jesus assures me that I am assailed, not by a single enemy, but by a legion of demons who surround me." And another time:—"My Mother, the demon oppresses me, crushes me as a person would who, having thrown a man to the ground, puts his knee on his breast to suffocate him."

On August 22, she had a vision which she records in a few words·—"I seemed to see the Holy Church—the Sovereign Pontiff, all the Bishops and Priests engaged in a great battle: everyone there had his portion of suffering. Our Lord explained to me that my sickness had also a mission. The devil was furious at this vision and ceased not to afflict me; but supported by obedience I remained firm." A little later she adds:—"Jesus speaks to me continually: He tells me ineffable things which He would have me write, but I feel too exhausted." One evening during Matins there was a tremendous storm: the hail fell with such violence that a great number of windows in our little Church and in the Monastery were broken. "My Mother," exclaimed our Sister, "what a frightful tempest! Well, the rage of the demon against me is like this."

Our dear Sister spent the 28th of August plunged in a sea of sorrow, interior and exterior, as our Lord had foretold to His Benjamin. It was about four o'clock in the afternoon when the supreme struggle commenced. We will pass in silence the details of these truly frightful hours, during which Jesus seemed to have abandoned His spouse to the power of the enemy. Her serene countenance so transformed as scarcely to be recognized, a prey to convulsive agitation, she repeated frequently as if under his influence "I am lost," and many other words which had never crossed her angelic lips. Rarely, we believe, does God permit His servants to be tried so far. The immense good that was to be effected by the example and writings of our dear Sister explains such an assault. But hell, in declaring itself openly against the elect spouse of our Lord, has only confirmed her celestial mission.

Nothing less than the presence of Monsignor our Bishop, and the holy exorcisms, had power to force Satan to leave his victim. But the hour of deliverance sounded at last. Toward midnight, Sister Benigna Consolata resumed her natural appearance; her sweet smile came back; and our Confessor having told her that during these terrible moments she ought to consider herself as the prisoner of the Heart of Jesus, condemned to remain in that Divine Heart for all Eternity, she cried out joyously:—"Benigna, prisoner of Jesus!"

During the following days there was a recurrence of these assaults but with less violence: a word of obedience, a pious hymn, or the suggestion of a holy thought sufficed to restore her to peace.

As soon as the conflict had ceased, Sister Benigna appeared to us *transfigured*. Her countenance shone with a childlike innocence so ravishing, that we could not look upon it without thinking of the *adorable features of the Infant Jesus*.

During her illness her abandonment, mortification and obedience were admirable. In its early stages she said to our Honored Mother: —"If Your Charity knew, my Mother, how Our Lord teaches me to practice mortification and not allow a single occasion to escape! At times when they bring me milk, I experience a strong repugnance, and Jesus wishes that I should take it with my most beautiful smile. At other times I am stifled with the heat and would like the fresh air; but the charitable Sister Infirmarian, seeing me in a perspiration, closes the curtain of the bed to protect me; nature is not pleased, but grace forces me to express my thanks. When my tired eyes would be glad of the darkness, they give me light; often one of our Sisters proposes to make my reading, when I would more willingly repose in silence to listen to the voice of Jesus: but He wishes that I should profit of every opportunity to mortify myself and renounce my own will."

The dear patient, being consumed with a burning fever and in consequence always thirsty, some refreshment was brought to her now and again, and at times ice. She said that when the Sister Infirmarian offered her the cup, if she had not held it, she would have swallowed the contents in a single draught; but through mortification she took it slowly and desisted after two spoonfuls. Our Mother inquiring why she did so, she replied:—"My Mother, our Lord stopped me, saying, This is enough, Nigna. After having taken the necessary relief, thou wilt only gratify nature." Our good Mother endeavored to protect her from the flies; but she graciously refused, saying that she might well support that little annoyance to honor the sufferings of Jesus, who on the Cross having His hands nailed, could not give Himself the least little relief.

She had the happiness of communicating every day. One morning during her thanksgiving she held her hands under the coverlet:— "Benigna," said Jesus, "put thy hands outside, and keep them joined, at least for some minutes; let no occasion escape of doing better, not to acquire merit, since thou must do all through love, but to glorify God." Once she cast a glance between the curtains of her bed to see one of our Sisters who was passing through the corridor; she reproached herself immediately and acknowledging it to our Mother, she added;—"In this moment so grave, when I am preparing to appear before the tribunal of God, I ought not to permit my self such satisfactions."

Our good Mother assisted her day and night, lavishing upon her the most delicate attentions. "My Mother," she said one morning after Holy Communion; "Our Lord has suggested a good practice of mortification; will you permit me to make it? O do not say no!"— "Yes," replied our Mother, "provided it does not aggravate your illness; what is it?"—"If Your Charity will permit, instead of absorbing the morsel of ice given to refresh me, I will hold it between my teeth; this will pain them; I will offer it to repair sacrileges, evil discourse, blasphemies and imprecations; it will be one suffering more, but Jesus gives me such a desire to suffer, that I would cry out; Lord, yet more! There remains so little time to live, that I may well bear pain without relief."

Our dear Sister was always docile to the prescriptions of the physicians. Obedient also to the Sister Infirmarian and to those who watched during the night, Sister Benigna Consolata asked for nothing, refused nothing. She never looked at the thermometer to note the degree which the fever had reached. Once she humbly accused herself of having unconsciously cast her eyes on the sheet which recorded the temperature, and which was near her bed.

Her brother, Signor Camillo Ferrero, came several times to see her during her illness; she was then conducted to the parlor in a little carriage. After his last visit the disease had made such great progress that this privilege had to be renounced. Her brother, therefore, while in the parlor wrote an affectionate farewell letter. When it was finished, our Mother hastened to bear it to the patient, who awaited it with sisterly impatience. She took the letter and opened it with joy, but immediately returned it to our Mother, saying: "Our Lord requires of me this sacrifice."—"But at least give me an answer for your brother, who is waiting."—"My Mother," replied our humble Sister, "do as Your Charity thinks proper; I feel that Jesus wills this proof of love from me." Habituated to sacrifice, this generous soul would have felt remorse had she let a single opportunity escape. Yet we know how tenderly she loved her relatives. During the last days of her life, in moments of delirium, she named them all with affection.

Her brother Camillo, as soon as he learned the gravity of her illness, asked and obtained from our Superiors, leave for a consultation with his cousin, Doctor Gurgo, professor of the Cottolengo Institute, Turin. Our physician willingly consented, and Doctor Gurgo soon arrived. The sight of her dear cousin recalled to Sister Benigna Consolata many sweet remembrances; she would naturally have desired to ask him many questions, to inquire about her beloved relatives, and give him affectionate messages for all; but, faithful to the inspirations of grace, she said not a word to gratify her desire, and contented herself with presenting him a little picture as a memory. The interior conflict and generous victory gained bv his cousin did not escape the keen eye of the eminent professor; he was profoundly edified, and in departing he said to our Honored Mother:—"What I have just seen does not astonish me; I have known Maria Consolata from her infancy, and I have always seen her practice extraordinary virtues." He afterward thanked our devoted doctor for the cares he had lavished upon the dear patient; the latter, on his side, expressed his admiration for the virtues of our angelic Sister.

"I know not even the name of my disease," she said at times; "this does not concern me. O what peace is in the *couper-court!* When the thought comes that such a thing would do me good, or that such another would do me harm, I cut it short instantly, saying, This does not concern me. Will my sufferings last a long time? When shall this martyrdom finish? Shall I preserve my consciousness to the end? This does not concern me. O how dear to Jesus is this abandonment in sickness! Nature shudders, but grace makes us say yes to all. I belong to myself no longer, I belong to Love! Without an extraordinary grace I could not bear smilingly so many sufferings at the same time; my heart throbs as if it would burst; my interior is all on fire; my shoulders sore and painful; my feet seem nailed to the bed. My eyes also have their special sufferings; now everything appears green, now a great light dazzles me, and again my head is besieged with all those thoughts that Your Charity knows. But it is justice; for every day of sickness has the mission of expiating the sins of a year of life."

Those thoughts of which our dear Sister speaks, were insinuated into her mind by the evil spirit. He tempted her to pride, to distrust, to despair. She baffled his wiles by discovering them to our venerated Ecclesiastical Superiors or to our Mother. When Her Charity was absent and the temptation returned, Sister Benigna Consolata humbly begged the Sister on watch to call her: "The enemy fears authority," she remarked, "and when our Mother is near me his assaults are less furious." At times the chanting of a pious hymn sufficed to divert the temptations of the demon, as formerly the melodious harp of David calmed the agitations of Saul.

After so many physical and moral sufferings, the great day of deliverance came at last for the privileged spouse of Jesus. On the 1st of September, which was the First Friday of the month, our edifying patient was able to receive for the last time the Holy Viaticum, after which she declined from hour to hour, preserving to the end her full consciousness. Frequently with great fervor she murmured the sacred names of Jesus and Mary. Toward half past one she recited with pain, but intelligibly, the act of contrition. At half past two our Confessor entered to renew the holy Absolution and recite the prayers for the Recommendation of the Departing Soul. At three o'clock, while she rested peacefully in the arms of our Mother, Sister Benigna Consolata opened her eyes suddenly, appeared to fix them on a distant and luminous point, and expired sweetly. The Confidant of Jesus had gone to be united to the Heart of her God!

The whole Community was present and profoundly afflicted at our loss. Our Confessor was finishing the *Subvenite* when our venerated Spiritual Father, who had so desired to assist at this blessed death, entered the room. He prayed a moment, then turning toward us, spoke words of comfort and fatherly affection to our grieving hearts. In the evening, Msgr. our Bishop came to kneel near our regretted Sister, who on her bed, surrounded with flowers and covered with a large white veil, resembled the virgins of the Catacombs, radiant with the glory of martyrdom. Far from inspiring fear, the Benjamin of Jesus attracted us sweetly to her; a celestial calm shone in her countenance; she seemed smiling at Eternal Love. A few days before her death she had said to some of our Sisters who were giving her their commissions for Heaven:—"I will send you treasures of happiness from Heaven." In fact, our grief for her loss was softened by a veritable effusion of joy, which sweetly dilated our hearts. Near her we seemed to be breathing the fragrance of Paradise.

Our good Bishop postponed the funeral till Sunday, September 3rd, that we might have the consolation of gazing longer on those angelic features. On that day he had the kindness to celebrate the Holy Mass in our little Church, and pronounce a eulogy on the religious virtues which had shone so conspiciously in that elect soul. His Lordship deigned to follow the modest funeral procession with the brother and sister of the deceased, both plunged in profound sorrow. The numberless testimonies of esteem given by our eminent Prelate to our regretted Sister Benigna Consolata made us feel still more our loss. May these unanimous regrets, we may say veneration, soften the affliction of these dear relatives, especially that of her father, and penetrate them with a holy pride for having given to the Church of God, in these sad times, such a religious as our Holy Founders desire:—"A daughter of sweet odor, of celestial colloquies."

The mortal remains of Sister Benigna Consolata repose, with our dear deceased Sisters in the cemetery of Camerlata. On her tomb, already the scene of pious pilgrimages, a white Cross extends its arms, and on it we read these words: *Alpha et Omega.*

Yes, Jesus was the beginning and the end of all her actions, the luminous pharos which conducted happily His little barque safe to the port.

May we imitate the virtues of our angelic Sister, and put in practice the divine instructions which remain to us a precious heritage; we shall thus become true Hosts consumed with the love of the Heart of Jesus.

DEUS LAUDETUR!

93

EXCERPTS FROM THE CIRCULAR OF THE

HONORED MOTHER JOSEPHINE ANTOINETTE SCAZZIGA,

Superior of the Visitation at Como, Lombardy from May, 1913, to May, 1919, the greater part of the Religious Life of Sister Benigna Consolata — Dated January 20th, 1919, and addressed to the HONORED MOTHERS OF THE ORDER

When for the first time, six years ago, God placed on my shoulders the heavy cross of Superiority, the contemplation of my weakness oppressed my soul with a mortal anguish· I felt absolutely wanting in those solid virtues required by this charge, as serious as delicate. Then descending into the centre of my nothingness, I embraced the holy Will of God, which takes pleasure in manifesting its power in misery, and I rose to Him with my only riches—the indigence of the poor............

The chosen flock which God intrusted to me from the hands of our never-to-be-forgotten Mother Maria Louisa Sobrero, inspired me at the same time with fear and hope. I aspired to make it more worthy of the favors of the Divine Lamb, yet I feared my incapacity. Taking refuge, nevertheless, under the mantle of the Immaculate Virgin Mary, our tender Mother, and ascending with her blessed aid to the most loving Heart of Jesus, I intrusted to Him this dear Community, and abandoned everything to His care............

Then calm was established in my soul............ My only solicitude was that the supernatural seeds sown by the Celestial Gardener in the souls of His dear spouses, should bring forth fruits. Not content with sowing the good grain, He caused it to spring up and ripen· His Heart, overflowing with love, rewarded my confidence with the happy experience that the more real my nothingness was, the more surely He would pour out His gifts in souls, and operate in them Himself.

Among all these dear Daughters, Jesus had reserved for me in His eternal designs, the Benjamin of His Heart, a precious jewel which, we believe, will increase "the humble glory" of our Visitation, and embellish the crown of our Holy Founders· The Abridgment of the Life and Virtues of our angelic Sister Benigna Consolata Ferrero has been sketched in broad outline; for the eagerness of all to know her, left us scarcely time to glean here and there, from the divine instructions of her Adorable Master. Nevertheless, the original Italian—already in its third edition, and spread rapidly from one extremity of our dear country to the other—gives a fair idea of her life to the reader. Besides the brevity imposed by circumstances, we deplore the impossibility of presenting the life to our beloved Houses until now in the language of the Institute.[1] Our dear Sisters of Montpellier, with most delicate and exquisite charity, offered to make a translation. We thank them anew for their great kindness, and take delight in the thought of the good their labor will produce, not only in our Order, but in elect pious souls, who will discover there the admirable effusions of the "Tendernesses" of the Divine Heart.

Esurientes implevit bonis. How incomparable is the sweetness of our God, how infinite His power! With empty hands we went to Him at the beginning of our government; and behold at the moment of being deposed from the Office, He loads us with riches! Ah, who will not confess that the soul that trusts in Him shall never be confounded!

It is with the precious *Vade Mecum,* the first diamond of so many treasures, that with emotion and gratitude, we embrace affectionately the Most Honored Mothers and Sisters of our dear Monasteries, who througout these six years have shown us so much affection. ....Through the hands of our venerated Mother Louise Eugénie Berard, we lay on the shrines of our Holy Founders the first copy of the *Vade Mecum,* translated and printed in French through the kindness of our dear Lyon-Fourviére......Our dear Holy Father and Mother will exult, we feel sure, since their dear Daughter Benigna of Jesus, truly "a daughter of good odor, a daughter of celestial colloquies." attained so high a degree of perfection and received such wonderful graces from the most sweet Heart of Jesus, only in consequence of her great fidelity in the exact observance of the holy Laws which they have given us. We intrust to our good God our debt of gratitude to this dear Monastery of Lyon-Fourviére, which has devoted itself with such cordial activity to insure a wider and easier circulation of His merciful "Tendernesses."

During the lifetime of our young Sister Benigna Consolata, we sought to accomplish the will of Jesus (*Pious Author*) by putting in print "The Way of the Cross," dictated, word for word, to His Benjamin. Immediately after her death, the Prayers, Decalogues,

---

[1]. The Circulars of the Order are in the French language.

95

and Maxims were added, and published under the title of VADE MECUM. If the work was hastened, it was only that in many places of the *Writings* of the *Little Secretary of Jesus,* souls might the sooner read how that loving Heart throbs with desire to make known to all the merciful manifestations of His love.

What shall we say to Your Charities of the sojourn among us of the new little Confidant of the Sacred Heart, heiress in this sense, of her immortal Elder Sister and Precursor, Margaret Mary, about to be crowned by the Holy Church with the aureole of the Saints; of her who, in a word, after the example of our Venerable Mother Mary de Sales Chappuis, attracts all hearts powerfully in the way of intimacy with the Saviour, a way which, in His merciful designs, is destined to assume a marvellous development in these modern times, steeped in materialism and indifference?.....Sweet and humble, tranquil and recollected, angelic in her demeanor as in her words, our Sister Benigna Consolata made it her supreme aim to efface herself in the sight of the Community. She succeeded so well that, while all admired her virtue, her Sisters were far from suspecting what treasures she kept jealously hidden in the depths of her heart. But when, on the 1st of September, 1916, the First Friday of the month, the passionate Lover of Jesus bade us adieu to go and abyss herself in His Adorable Heart, the perfumes of the broken alabaster vase were shed with such profusion that "the whole house was embalmed." Then they learned the affluence of celestial favors, of marvellous graces, and above all, of solid virtues, that adorned that beautiful soul. The precious balm was propagated, not only among our dear neighboring Communities, but to those in far distant regions. The death of this humble child was indeed a complete revelation. Here she has left us, in a very special manner, a powerful stimulus to strive to rejoin her in her way of confidence, intimacy and love.

We solicit your spiritual assistance most earnestly for our zealous Ananias, the Very Reverend Canon D. Antonio Piccinelli, recently exalted to the dignity and title of Msgr. the Vicar General of this vast Diocese. His profound humility had not power to keep his merit hidden, as he desired and the choice of our Bishop fell upon him. Although by this appointment the field of his labors will be considerably enlarged, our venerated Prelate will continue with wonderful kindness to exercise among us his fatherly ministries. (It will be remembered that this saintly Father was Confessor and Guide to Sister Benigna Consolata during her whole religious life, and that God made known to her his sanctity several times in a supernatural manner.)

AFTERWORD.

THREE YEARS have scarcely glided by since our angelic Sister Benigna Consolata took her flight to her Beloved; yet we may say without exaggeration that her name, her humble writings, are already known to the world. From the remote regions of America, Ireland, England, even from the coasts of Africa, come continual requests for a brief life of the Sister and some of her writings; and not infrequently we receive joyous communications of favors obtained through her protection,—cures and other helps attributed by pious souls to her intervention.

In truth, people are pressing and insistent in their demands for her precious writings, her picture, and the little "VADE MECUM", as well as leaflets bearing excerpts from her "Journal," translated into French, English and Spanish, which are being rapidly diffused. This humble Religious so avid of the hidden life, of being buried in the lowly ways of humility and self-effacement, shines today with a splendor so striking, an attractiveness so sweet, that everywhere her picture or brief passages from her writings, draw souls to her with bonds so potent and irresistible, that they are prompted to invoke her intercession. Her efficacious assistance is felt by all. So well this dear Religious keeps her promise of making herself all to all; that charity whose ardent flame consumed her soul on earth, is made perfect today in the enjoyment of her God, and she finds her delight in consoling whoever has recourse to her.

The graces so obtained are already innumerable and diverse, both in the spiritual and temporal order. As to the first, we may signalise the solving of many painful problems, the removal of difficulties, anguish of mind dispelled as if by enchantment, and consoling conversions to God. We see peace and tranquillity restored to troubled hearts; confidence and love establishing their empire on the ruins of distrust and fear; and, above all, numerous germs of religious vocations unfolding, thanks to the influence of this beloved of the Divine Heart. Sister Benigna Consolata is a sweet and prompt benefactor, who cannot resist the supplications of afflicted and confiding souls.

Here follow in the record of our Sisters of Como, several pages narrating cures and other favors which have been obtained through the intercession of the "Little Secretary of Jesus" during the years since her death in various provinces of Italy and in adjoining countries.

May we not cherish an unfailing confidence that Sister Benigna Consolata, Apostle of the Mercy of Jesus, will exert the plenitude of her influence over His Sacred Heart in favor of our own dear country? May we not induce her to scatter over our United States some of the treasures which Jesus has given her to distribute? And her holy example—is it not destined to stimulate faithful souls to a more exalted perfection and union with God by the way of sacrifice He taught her; to draw souls from the darkness of unbelief and the corruption of vice; to lay bare to tempted souls the snares of the evil spirit, and deliver them, through the promises made her by Jesus after her own frequent and astounding victories over the malign enemy?

We cannot forbear giving to our readers a letter from an eminent ecclesiastic, which speaks volumes in favor of the seraphic Nun whose brief career on earth has been marked with such extraordinary effusions of divine grace. It is from the hand of the Reverend Father J. B. Lemius, former Superior of the Chaplains of Mont martre, renowned for learning and piety, and especially for his extraordinary devotion to the Sacred Heart of Jesus. It was written to her whose wise and loving direction urged Sister Benigna Consolata ever forward up the steeps of sanctity, the Honored Mother Josephine Antoinette Scazziga of Como.

My very Honored Mother,

The Sacred Heart of Jesus overflows with love and mercy at this turning point in the History of the Church, and stimulates us more than ever to confidence and love.

The Visitation remains the chosen organ to repeat to the world the sweet appeals, the ineffable promises of the Divine Master, and the heartrending cries of His unappreciated tenderness.

The dear Sister Benigna Consolata Ferrero, of Como, affords a new proof of this divine mission.

How ravishing and consoling are the pages of the *Vade Mecum*, first of the writings dictated by the *Pious Author*, whom we invoke by saying; *Pie Jesu!* The Canon Saudreau, our acknowledged Master in Mysticism, writes me that he recognizes the accent of Our Lord, as we recognize the accent of a traveler from a foreign land.

Authoritative voices, I trust, will encourage you; zealous souls of all countries will aid you in passing from hand to hand, and in spreading everywhere the celestial writings of the privileged Secretary of the Sacred Heart. Poor sinners will not be afraid to throw themselves into the arms of the Merciful Jesus; pious souls in the world and in the cloister will no longer find an obstacle to love.

May we be favored without delay with the holy life and all the works of the sweet Benigna!

I am most grateful to you, my very Honored Mother, for having made her known to me. Accept the expression of my religious devotedness in the Sacred Heart.

J. B. LEMIUS.

Bordeaux, February 27, 1919.

Conformably to the decrees of Urban VIII, we declare that we attribute a purely human belief alone to all that is contained in this biography.

THE CONTENTS.

62197258R00059

Made in the USA
Columbia, SC
30 June 2019